LIFE HAPPENS.
Live Anyway.

A MEMOIR of
SURVIVAL and SUCCESS.

Dr. Sheryl Kenan Randolph

Nashville, Tennessee

Unless otherwise indicated, Scripture quotations are from the ESV® Bible (The Holy Bible, English Standard Version®), copyright © 2001 by Crossway Bibles, a publishing ministry of Good News Publishers. Used by permission. All rights reserved.

Scripture marked NKJV are taken from the New King James Version. Copyright © 1982 by Thomas Nelson, Inc. Used by permission. All rights reserved.

Life Happens. Live Anyway.
Copyright © 2020 by Sheryl Kenan Randolph
All rights reserved.

Published by Juniper Rockwell
Nashville, Tennessee
juniperrockwell.com

Library of Congress Control Number: 2020918961

ISBN 978-0-578-76730-7 (Paperback)
ISBN 978-0-578-76736-9 (eBook)

Cover photograph by Harlan Keith Breaux
Book design by Linwood Hawkins Jr.

For more information about the author, visit sherylrandolph.com

To the amazing people who choose to LIVE
regardless of their circumstances.

To Mother Gatlin, you have been such a positive influence in my life both spiritually and naturally. Thank you for demonstrating what a real prayer life should be — I will be forever grateful to you. Enjoy this book from Pastor Kenan's daughter and know that you are genuinely loved!

Love Always
Jeva Nolly
- 2020

Contents

Introduction — vii

1. When The Unexpected Happens — 1
   Surround Yourself With Purposeful People

2. When Betrayal Happens — 15
   Practice Forgiveness

3. When Exhaustion Happens — 27
   Perform Self-Care

4. When Success Happens — 37
   Stay Humble And Focus On God

5. When Duality And Doubt Happen — 55
   Know Your Worth

6. When Loss Happens — 67
   Accept What God Allows

7. When Failure Happens — 79
   Be Honest With Yourself

8. When Depression Happens — 91
   Ask For Help

9. When "The End" Happens — 103
   Let Go And Move Forward

10. When Trials And Tribulations Happen — 116
    Find Strength Through Your Faith

11. When Victory Happens — 129
    Praise God And Pour Into Others

Acknowledgments — 137

Introduction

I often thank God for the difficulties in my life.

That sounds strange, right? I mean, who really *enjoys* the stress of figuring out how to pay a past-due electricity bill when there's no cash in their bank account, or who gladly welcomes the physical pain and debilitation caused by chronic illness? I am a pastor, education consultant, inspirational speaker and life coach. A large portion of my time each day is spent encouraging others who feel devastated by life's challenges. And I must say, I rarely encounter people who delight in their defeat or rejoice when their hearts are broken.

I'll confess; the thought of reliving my darkest days does not excite me either. Not even in the slightest bit! But it's through those hard times that God truly received my full and undivided attention. I learned to trust Him, lean on Him and be still while He worked. I became intimately acquainted with the idea that sometimes He will tear things all the way down to the foundation in order to rebuild again.

I am the poster child for rebuilding, bouncing back and rebounding. My closest friends will tell you they don't know how, but it seems I always manage to get up after being knocked down, dust off and proceed to live intentionally and victoriously every day. There's no magic pill I take that replenishes my strength and gives me the will to carry on. I don't have a private stash of "joy juice" that keeps me going. In fact, many times I wasn't sure if I'd ever recover from the blows that should have kept me down for the count.

The reality is actually quite simple, and nothing is magical about it: when confronted with life's numerous trials, I've learned how to *choose* optimism, positivity and victory. It certainly has not been easy, and it's no secret that I could never accomplish this alone. God blessed me with the gift of being a natural-born optimist, and He placed countless people on my path who helped pick me up time and time again throughout my journey.

Today, I gain strength in sharing my struggles. Telling you about the trials I overcame means I made it through them! I am winning! And I know there is still more triumph in store for me. It is my hope that I can help someone else with what I've learned, and I can be a testament to the basic principle that our trials make us stronger. In addition to being my personal story, this book is a toolkit for navigating adversity. Each chapter contains specific guidance, scriptures and prayers to help you move forward after difficult situations and hardships. I am eager for us to stand together in victory!

LIFE HAPPENS

There is a season and a time for everything. And while all of God's plans for my future are yet to be revealed, sometimes I feel as though I've already experienced the full weight of *everything* throughout my five decades on this earth. I've certainly had my share of exceptional highs and tremendous lows on this rollercoaster called life. Success like leading a church through years of exponential growth was fulfilling beyond my wildest imagination. Receiving acclaim from my peers during my 23-year career as an educator was also rewarding. My greatest success ever – raising two beautiful children who have become thriving young adults – has brought more joy to my life than I ever knew was possible.

On the other hand, life has kicked me in the teeth many times over. It's happened so much that I'm frequently asked, "Pastor Sheryl, how are you always so positive, even in negative situations? If anyone deserves to host a spectacular pity party, it's you!" It's true; when enduring the embarrassment of a public scandal that threatened my marriage, putting a smile on my face was the last thing I wanted to do. When witnessing my mother – my best friend – fight for her life, there were days I wanted to call it quits, throw in the towel and give up.

It's not hard to identify with the emotional responses that are associated with ups and downs. It's the nature of our universal human experience. We laugh, and we cry; we party, and we mourn; we are born, and we inevitably die; and all that happens in between is called "life." It's a difficult phenomenon to quickly define. Life is a collection of experiences, memories and relationships, and its meaning has been pondered since the beginning of time. It inspires art, it compels us to seek purpose and, for those of us in the faith community, it serves as our opportunity to glorify our Creator as He leads us to our destiny.

However you define it, life will undoubtedly surprise us and take us places we were not expecting to go. Even more sobering, it will take us where we don't *want* to go. As much as we would like for there to be, there are no shortcuts to our destinations. And that's what this book is about. What happens when we have to walk through trials that feel like they're going to take us all the way out? What are we to do when our world is turned upside down and inside out? What recourse do we have when the pillars of our lives start to crumble? We won't always know the form in which our trials will manifest themselves – i.e. financially, medically, or even relationally – but we know they are coming because it's just part of the deal; we must accept the bad with all the good we receive. What we do know is that we can prepare for what's coming and be ready to face it head on with the power of God on our side.

What Does It Mean To "Live Anyway?"

"Most people die at age 25 and don't get buried until they are 65."

The first time I heard this quote by author and speaker Les Brown, it stuck with me. His message encouraged living a full life instead of merely existing; there's a huge difference. Rather than just going through the motions of life's obligatory daily duties, take risks, explore, love, and make good use of each minute you are given. How you choose to "live anyway" may look different from your neighbor, but the *choice* to live is the same!

The deeper question that occurred to me was, *What causes people to stop living? What stifles their joy and stunts their growth?* I imagine there are a myriad of answers to those questions. Perhaps a traumatic occurrence, or maybe a general loss of faith in humanity. Regardless of the cause, I believe there is a common solution: we must recognize where and how we lost our way, recalibrate and find the courage to live with purpose and passion.

If you are like me, then you daydreamed about your future when you were a child.

Growing up as a Southern belle in Midland, Texas, I was raised in a two-parent home by my father William Kenan, a Pentecostal pastor, and my mother Bertha Lee Kenan, his first lady and life partner. My social and spiritual norms were conservative, innocent and, frankly, simple. God was the head of our household, my father was our leader, my mother his helpmate, and the four children – my two sisters, my brother and I – were obedient preacher's kids. We attended church five days a week and kept a very busy schedule. My parents traveled a lot and there was always church-related work to be done. Sundays, however, were our special time when we had family dinners. The Sundays that my mother didn't cook, we went to Furr's, a cafeteria-style restaurant, where I enjoyed my favorite dishes: sirloin, mashed potatoes, green beans and apple pie. We'd eat, laugh and talk during this short break between morning and afternoon worship services. During our formative years, these dinners were a staple tradition that bonded us together for a lifetime.

Our nuclear family unit was vitally important because none of our other relatives lived in Texas. My maternal grandmother, who lived in Newark, New Jersey, visited us every Christmas. I affectionately called her Minnie Pearl. She was the coolest granny and always wore fashionable hats to match every outfit. My dad's parents lived on a farm in Rose Hill, North Carolina, and we visited them in the summers. Our grandparents often teased that my sisters and I were "city girls" who got our church shoes dirty while walking in the fields and watching them chop tobacco.

For me, life as a child was peaceful, balanced, centered and carefree. My 12-year-old assessments of the world were formed through loving, hopeful and spiritual lenses. My aspirations for my future followed suit. I dreamed of being a professional singer. My sisters and I wanted to be "The Famous Kenan Sisters," much like the Clark Sisters, nationally renowned gospel singers. I dreamed I'd fall in love with a Christian man – specifically a minister – and become a preacher's wife. I wanted to grow up to be like my mother, married for 40 years to a loving, faithful husband, raising a house full of children, who we'd teach to serve the Lord by example and by studying scripture. My parents would delight in their grandchildren and pass along the wisdom only they could. That was my dream; my happily ever after.

The only problem is, fairytales rarely come true. When I hit adulthood, I got a rude awakening and experienced a series of life-altering events that almost broke me: Illness reared its ugly head; betrayals occurred; depression arrived; family dynamics changed; and the devil emptied his bag of tricks to try to bring me down.

Through it all, I learned that it's not so much *what* you are dealing with, but more about how you *react* to it. We have choices. We can choose to wallow in self-pity. We can choose to live in a state of denial. We can accept abuse, insecurity and resentment. Or we can be confident in knowing our worth, fight for our lives, practice forgiveness and stand triumphantly over our trials.

If you have been devastated by life in any way, then I want you to know you can not only survive, but you can thrive in the aftermath. When you encounter difficult moments in life, I want to help you make destiny decisions and not detrimental decisions. I want to help you bounce back and strengthen your belief system so you can live better and not bitter.

Our ultimate survival is in the Lord, and our *best* path in life is through Him. But this book is for both people of faith and those who are not. I hope to never be so heavenly-minded that I'm no earthly good and unable to reach those who do not share my beliefs. I am confident that the stories and guidance throughout these chapters can offer universal inspiration to those who read them. They will also illuminate why I trust Him to guide my life.

This book is to help you understand that there is life after challenging and difficult situations. This is your go-to guide that says, *When life is really rough, these instructions are how to choose to live anyway.* What looks and feels devastating, doesn't have to devastate you. Just because something brought you to your knees, you don't have to stay there. Life will change you, but it doesn't have to break you. God does not bring us through the valley so that we can merely exist. On the contrary, He wants us to live.

SCRIPTURE AND PRAYER

Count it all joy, my brothers, when you meet trials of various kinds, for you know that the testing of your faith produces steadfastness. And let steadfastness have its full effect, that you may be perfect and complete, lacking in nothing.

James 1:2-4

For I know the plans I have for you, declares the Lord, plans for welfare and not for evil, to give you a future and a hope.

Jeremiah 29:11

Let's pray together

Faithful Father,

Thank You for never leaving my side. Through all of life's celebrations and challenges, You have always been with me. Because of You, I will not be shaken, whatever life throws at me. Please continue to guide my path and protect me from powerful forces that arise against me.

As I experience the brokenness of this world, refresh my soul each day with Your perfect and complete peace. I will boldly praise Your name and confidently live my life in the light of Your love, no matter what might be happening around me.

There is no God like You, and You are worthy of all my praise.

Through Jesus Christ, our Lord, I pray. Amen.

1

When The Unexpected Happens
Surround Yourself With Purposeful People

The call we'd been waiting for finally came. My husband was formally invited to serve in ministry at a Pentecostal church in Chattanooga, Tennessee. The church leadership made an offer to relocate my husband and me from Midland, Texas, and we were more than ready to set out on a new adventure. Having been married only one year, we were still in honeymoon bliss. We were eager to take on the world and build our legacy together.

A mutual friend of ours was a pastor with several locations across the Southeast including churches in South Carolina, Florida and Tennessee. He was unable to replicate himself across all of them and asked my husband to be the assisting pastor at the Tennessee location. If everything went well, my husband would be permanently assigned as the site pastor. This opportunity fit our vision as a couple and was the answer to our prayers. My husband could curtail his extensive evangelism travel schedule and increase his income at the same time. And as a young couple, we could put down roots and start a family.

We accepted the offer.

At the time, I was an assistant principal in the Midland Independent School District and was on track to becoming a principal. My young career in education was off to a great start, but I would have to transition to a new environment with my upcoming move to Tennessee. The only thing I knew about Chattanooga was the song "Chattanooga Choo Choo," but being newly married and in love, I embraced the unknown with optimism. Also, I was a preacher's daughter, so the life of church ministry was familiar territory. I believed this shift into the role of being a pastor's wife would come to me very naturally. My whole life I'd watched my mother operate as one of the greatest first ladies and administrative assistants I'd ever seen. So, I felt equipped; I was in my comfort zone. It was divine providence. I could see God's plan coming together and my husband and I were ready to walk in our destiny. So, I started to do my part to make the move successful. I started planning for our arrival in Tennessee.

I coordinated with the church administrator who offered to assist with our living arrangements and made recommendations on which apartment complexes in Chattanooga might be suitable for us. I communicated to our landlord in Midland that we would not be renewing our lease and I started packing. I shared the details of our move with my family – who was happy to see things falling into place for me, but was sad that I'd be living 16 hours away – and I began an extensive job search for an administrative position in the Chattanooga school system.

There were definitely moments when I felt anxiety about the move. It was likely a combination of excitement and nervousness. But I found comfort in the planning process. I felt as long as we were organized and methodically prepared, we should be fine. If we completed every checklist, dotted all our Is and crossed all our Ts, then everything should go smoothly.

As our move drew closer, my husband and I made final preparations.

"Sheryl, we'll buy a ticket for you to fly to Nashville since it's cheaper than flying directly into Chattanooga," he said. "Then, we'll arrange a car ride to Chattanooga from there. Since I have some other evangelism opportunities, I'll take the car to conduct these revivals and drive to Chattanooga when I'm done. We should arrive about the same time."

The move to Tennessee was going to require some sacrifices – like being away from my husband for what I expected to be a short time and starting over in a new school system – but I thought to myself: *This is marriage. I'm in love. We're on our way to our new adventure in life. It's going to be great!*

Despite meticulous planning to relocate to Tennessee and join the local faith community, the transition was quite rocky. What started out as an exciting launch into my new life with my husband quickly turned into one of the first trials of my young adulthood.

In the summer of 1996, my flight landed in Nashville, Tennessee. Although I wasn't thrilled to be arriving alone, I was excited to be one step closer to my new home.

Sister Linda, one of the ladies from my new church home, picked me up from the airport. We'd never met in person, so I had no clue what she looked like. But I was hoping I'd know her when I saw her. I was a 27-year-old, conservative church girl bouncing down the terminal walkway dressed in a long skirt down to my ankles, suntan stockings, white socks and sneakers. Linda picked me out of the crowd right away.

"You must be Sheryl Randolph," she said.

"I am! And are you Sister Linda?!" I was elated to connect with someone with whom I had familiarity.

"Yes, it's me," she said. We hugged as if we were old friends, I loaded my luggage in the car and we set out on our two-hour drive from Nashville to Chattanooga. Prior to meeting in person, Linda and I had talked via phone every week during my preparations to move to Chattanooga. She did everything in her power to make my arrival as smooth as possible. Unfortunately, there were some immediate hiccups that were outside of her control.

The church assisted with securing living quarters for me and my husband by arranging a meeting with the apartment complex manager, but the deposit for our unit had not been paid. A series of miscommunications and erroneous expectations resulted in my move-in day being put on hold, and I found myself in Chattanooga without a "home." In addition to the deposit, both my husband's and my signature were required on the lease. He had yet to arrive in town due to delays in his schedule, a frequent occurrence as he regularly traveled around the country to conduct revivals.

For my first month in Chattanooga, I lived in a hotel as I waited for my husband to join me. I used my credit card to pay the hotel bills when I ran out of cash. When we had our daily check-in phone conversations, I always tried to exude a positive and supportive spirit.

"Honey, we can manage this," I reassured my husband. "How are things going with you? When are you getting here?"

"I'll be there as soon as I can," he said. "I have to take advantage of these evangelism opportunities as they come." My husband was trying to generate some additional revenue during the summer months before his official position at the church started in August. I didn't want to further aggravate the situation and question why his extended travel schedule wasn't resulting in more money that he could send me to get our affairs squared away in our new city. So, I soldiered on without complaining.

I was sad and frustrated that things weren't going according to plan. What was supposed to be a synchronized arrival turned into me not laying eyes on my husband for nearly two months. While I lived in a city 1,100 miles from home surrounded by people I didn't know, I had no money and no permanent place to live. That was not the plan at all! As hard as it was, I knew I had to stay optimistic while God worked things out.

Things on the job front were not going as expected either. When agreeing to move to Chattanooga, I was promised an in-person interview for an assistant principal position with Chattanooga City Public Schools. My interviews over the phone had all but sealed the deal, and only the formalities of signing the paperwork remained. However, when I showed up to claim the position, it mysteriously was no longer a good "fit" for me. I'll never forget my conversation with the human resources representative who retracted the offer.

"Sweetie, we thought we had an assistant principal position for you, but as it turns out, we don't," the human resources representative said. "However, there is a teaching position that is more fitting for you. I'll connect you with the principal of the school where the opening is."

I was baffled by this inexplicable change of circumstance. My phone interviews prior to my move had gone tremendously well, but my in-person meeting was falling flat. With the other snags and bumps that had already derailed my "smooth" relocation, a monkey wrench in my job situation was the last thing I needed. So, I pushed back.

"No ma'am! I moved to Tennessee to be an assistant principal; to be in administration," I sternly reminded her.

"It's just not right for you," she rebutted. "But you're very young. If you just hang in there and work your way up, in about five years or so, you'll be ready."

Again, I countered. "So, on the phone, I was the one you had been searching for and your 'answer to prayer.' In person, I'm not 'ready'?!"

I thought I recognized what was happening here. I never want to accuse anyone of something as ugly as racism, ageism, or sexism, but I couldn't come up with any other explanation for why I was now underqualified and unprepared for the job. My professionalism, resume, experience and accolades spoke volumes during my numerous *blind* phone interviews, but being a young, black, female sitting in front of the HR representative's face seemed to drown out the former. I think they were willing to tolerate my gender and check one "diversity" box. But to be female, black and young?! Heaven forbid that I'd be bold enough to be all three at the same time!

It didn't help that the message was delivered by another woman who happened to be older and Caucasian. It was almost as if her attitude was, *I've arrived and I've "made it." But, you? You haven't paid your dues. And you expect to sashay in here and go straight to the top? Oh no, not today.*

I had somewhat experienced discrimination in Midland, but it was never so bold. I was definitely in a new world now and struggled to find my place.

I realized in that moment that life is full of unexpected twists and turns, and I had to develop a strategy for staying on course.

I quickly learned that when you encounter the unexpected, no matter how big or small your situation is, it's important to be flexible and open to alternative ideas. Going it alone and trying to accomplish all your tasks on your own is not ideal. Surrounding yourself with solution-focused people can help you keep moving forward. Surrounding yourself with purposeful people allows others to share your burden. We all need community to survive. We need a village to thrive.

For me, my village began to develop very soon after I arrived in Chattanooga. Silver linings started to appear in the clouds that had stormed all over my parade. Thank God, there were people placed on my path who helped me along the way.

Although my employment situation was in limbo, fortunately for me, my newfound friend Linda was a special education teacher for Chattanooga City Public Schools. She knew I had a masters degree and a background in special education, and she was instrumental in helping me secure employment with the school system. She clued me in about the positions that were frequently available, and helped me get my foot in the door.

After a few more interviews, instead of the assistant principal job I originally expected, I received an offer for a teaching position working with children who had been diagnosed emotionally disturbed at a local middle school. When I finally proved that I secured a job, the management at the apartment complex accepted my sole signature on the lease agreement, along with a $500 deposit, and I was able to move in.

It was the first time in my life I'd ever lived alone. Even though I had left home to attend Oral Roberts University in Tulsa, Oklahoma, I had a roommate while I was there. After college, I went back home to live with my parents in Midland until I met my husband and got an apartment with him. Now, contrary to our best laid plans, I was by myself.

To make matters worse, I arrived in Chattanooga before the moving truck that had all our furniture and belongings from Midland. The trucking company was waiting for the second half of its payment – which I could not afford to pay – and refused to deliver our belongings until it was paid. This was the result of another epic communication failure among the new church, my husband and me. I was in an apartment with no furniture and no bed, my husband had the car that we shared, and my whole life was packed up in a truck that was parked somewhere between Texas and Tennessee. I wasn't working yet, but the cash I spent on the apartment deposit, plus my savings, were supposed to sustain me until my husband arrived.

Many nights, I sat on the floor with my legs crossed and watched a small TV that I had borrowed and propped up on a storage crate. I ate peanut butter and crackers for dinner, and feelings of abandonment, loneliness and confusion often brought me to tears. I did not understand how my situation turned out so differently than I had planned. My pride prevented me from calling home. Besides, I didn't want my parents to worry about me.

Slowly, things started falling into place and working in my favor. As God had it, my apartment ended up being three blocks away from the school where I would be teaching. That was perfect because the assistant principal role I initially wanted was located across town, and I didn't have a car.

Sister Linda became my rock. She got up early every day and took me to work at 7 a.m. She arrived at my apartment complex every morning like clockwork with rollers in her hair and wearing her lounging gown. While she was also a teacher, classes started at 9 a.m. at her school. She'd pick me up, take me to work, then return home to get herself dressed. She also picked me up and brought me to church every Sunday. And if ever she was unable to chauffer me, she'd arrange for someone else to drive me.

Linda felt bad that I was alone, and she went above and beyond to help me be comfortable. She bought me blankets and an air mattress to help make my empty apartment a little more livable. And the ladies from the church gifted me pots and pans so I could cook.

I can only smile when I think about the first time the church mothers took me to the grocery store. "We're going to take you shopping," they said. "Get all you want. Get you some ribs, steak, chicken, whatever you see that you like."

These people are so sweet, I said to myself. I was so grateful for the assistance and very much looked forward to breaking bread with my new church members.

At the register, the ladies from the church pooled their financial resources together to get me what I needed. Linda must have seen the humbled look on my face because she leaned in close to me and said, "Sheryl, the saints are here to bless you. Let them help."

This experience took my mind back to when I was exposed to the concept of receiving assistance early in life. There were free lunch programs at my elementary school. My young mind couldn't process everything that was happening back then; but when casually surveying the lunch line, my siblings and I "paid" for lunch with big blue tickets and everybody else used little pink tickets. To this day, I don't know which color entitled one to a "free" lunch.

There's absolutely no shame in accepting help, and I'm forever in debt to those who saw my need and chose to pour their resources into me. Some of the worst of times were turned into the best of times because of great company and cheerful givers. The steak dinners weren't too bad, either.

There were others who stepped in and helped me out while I waited for my husband to join me in Chattanooga. One of many examples was Robert, a fellow teacher who befriended me. We first met when he saw me walking home after work one day.

"Girl, where are you going?" he asked as he pulled his car over to the curb of a busy highway where I was walking on the edge of the road.

"I'm walking home to my apartment," I responded.

"Get off this street!" he admonished me. "You're cute and young; somebody might snatch you up. Get in this car!"

That was our first introduction. From that day forward, he showed me the ropes at school, helped me get acclimated to my new job and most graciously drove me home every day. We would have the best times in our afternoon ride home. Robert educated me about the political landscape of Chattanooga, specifically the school system. We listened to country music and shared stories about our hometowns. He told me that Chattanooga was a good city, and encouraged me to stick it out because he believed I would do well here.

Robert and I were the true epitome of the phrase "opposites attract." I was a black, church girl and he was a Caucasian, free-spirited man. We didn't share all of the same beliefs – which many times influences a person's behavior. He knew I was in ministry and didn't buy into some of the teachings. "I don't agree with all that religiosity that y'all do in church," he frankly expressed. "But Sheryl, you're one of the first people in ministry who does not judge me, and I truly appreciate your friendship."

"Robert, you're good people," I replied. "You were kind to me when others simply watched me walk home or watched me fumble my way through my new job. Your friendship is priceless to me." He was one of the kindest, smartest people I had met, and we remained close as we moved through the ranks of the school system.

We were drawn together by our commonalities of decency, kindness and compassion. We rejected the idea that our differences in faith and background prohibited us from simply being good human beings toward one another. We accepted each other without precondition and had honest dialogue that others may have considered off-limits. We took care of each other and had lots of fun in the process.

When The Unexpected Happens
Live Anyway
Surround Yourself With Purposeful People

- **Build Your Village.** Surround yourself with supportive and purposeful people who will love you without judging, who will always tell you the truth and who have honest conversations with you that others may think are taboo. Build your village and rely on them. Develop a group of like-minded people who can make bad times better simply with their presence. Seek people who are responsible, disciplined and offer wise advice. It also helps people to know that they matter in your life. People who love you want to help, and they get joy from lending their support.

- **Let Others Share Your Burdens.** Sometimes walking in your purpose is full of pain, but that does not give you permission to abandon it. God will send people to walk beside you in difficult places; be humble enough to accept the escort when it is needed. In Exodus 18:17-23, God taught Moses that he should not try to do everything by himself. He taught him the importance of delegating tasks to others so he would not wear himself out. Recognize when it's not time to be a loner, and let people help you. When you isolate yourself and try to do everything on your own, it leads to exhaustion. God puts people in your life for a reason and it does not make you less of a parent, less of a leader, or less of a person to rely on them. Great people understand the power of seeking and accepting help; they know it is not an indication of weakness, rather it is an indication of strength.

- **Be Open to Receiving Help From Unexpected Places.** Be receptive of the idea that your support may come from someone who is of a different race, gender or belief system. When we embrace friendships from unexpected places, we begin to understand that we typically have more in common with others than what may initially meet the eye. If we judge others instead of accepting our differences, then we may miss an opportunity to meet a new friend. Jesus never shied away from people who didn't share his beliefs or agree with his teachings, in fact, he actively approached them and showed them love.

- **Sow What You Seek To Reap.** I believe it's important to be the type of person you want to attract in your life. When you are kind, helpful and giving to others, it puts you in a place where people don't mind helping you. Make sure you are a giver, and you will find yourself receiving and walking in the harvest of your sown seeds. Always display a spirit of positivity, do unto others as you would have them do to you, and you will discover people who are eager and honored to offer their assistance.

SCRIPTURE AND PRAYER

Two are better than one, because they have a good reward for their toil. For if they fall, one will lift up his fellow. But woe to him who is alone when he falls and has not another to lift him up!

———

Ecclesiastes 4:9-10

Listen to advice and accept instruction, that you may gain wisdom in the future. Many are the plans in the mind of a man, but it is the purpose of the Lord that will stand.

———

Proverbs 19:20-21

Dear God,

Thank You for kindness that goes beyond family and reaches out to strangers. When I was in need, You placed people on my path who responded to that need even though I was unable to return the favor. They helped me operate in wisdom and offered practical, everyday advice and assistance. Thank You for those who go the extra mile, and even when it is a sacrifice for them, they choose to obey Your voice and live out a purpose bigger than themselves.

Please forgive me when I try to do life all on my own. Forgive me for trying to walk in pride especially when I know I need help. Continue to grant me humility to accept the help that You provide.

God, teach me to navigate through daily life and find my way through negative situations so that they don't smother and kill me. Help me to seek, find and discern those people who are divinely and purposefully connected to my destiny. I don't want to be around negative people; I know that fools will teach me how to live for a day, but wise people will help me survive for a lifetime. Equip me with a proper people detector to inform me of who is purposeful for every situation and every season. Amen.

2

When Betrayal Happens
Practice Forgiveness

My husband arrived in Chattanooga about eight weeks after I did. After two months of constant problem solving, negotiating and adjusting to a foreign environment without my spouse, I was relieved to finally have him home. It was comforting to know I no longer had to hold down the fort alone. Our reunion was refreshing and, at last, we were able to settle into our new lives. He officially became a member of the church leadership staff and I began my job as a special education teacher at the middle school.

My husband was serving in a role at the church that can best be described as a managing site pastor. He filled the gaps when the senior pastor was evangelizing in other cities or visiting one of the other congregations he led. My husband preached sermons on Sunday mornings, led Bible study on Wednesday nights, managed some of the ministries, and participated in the daily operations. I was right by his side pitching in wherever I could, singing in the choir and working with the ministers' wives. We had limited authority to spearhead any significant changes in the church, but we were more like appointed stewards for maintaining order and providing leadership for the approximately 300 members while the senior pastor was away.

When he would return to town, we'd take a back seat and observe the display of allegiance and love between him and the parishioners. The congregation's staunch loyalty to its pastor was palpable and unwavering. Even still, he said he wanted to slowly and strategically transition my husband to lead pastor, and me, first lady.

"I'm going to leave you all in charge while I'm gone," he instructed. "But we have to be careful. I want to make sure we get you all into the heart of the people. I envision you all leading this congregation, but the people won't take too kindly to it yet."

What the pastor did not count on was the people taking such a liking to us right away.

My husband's charisma was a gift from God that mesmerized the congregation. The people loved him and were drawn to him like a magnet. He was a great orator and presenter, he dressed well, could sing, and was an overall likeable person; a full package. Some of the parishioners even began referencing him as "Pastor" Randolph instead of "Elder" Randolph. And I was his suitable complement; a warm and bubbly, Southern girl from Texas. People constantly praised, "Oh, she is so sweet. And she can sing! They are both just wonderful."

As quickly as our popularity began to rise, so did our problems. Our time of being the "darlings" of the church was short-lived, and what had the potential of being a successful transition of leadership – with the blessing of the senior pastor – suddenly became threatened by symptoms of jealousy, insecurity and animosity.

At first, the critiques were subtle, and could even be laughed off as harmless ribbing of the "new guys."

"Pastor, Elder Randolph is trying to take over your church!" a church member would say to the senior pastor about my husband. "As a matter of fact, he didn't even acknowledge you this Sunday."

Then, my joy and passion for singing in the church choir became a source of controversy. Admiration of my singing started with comments like, "Lady Randolph can really sing; we want to hear more of her!" That enthusiasm inexplicably soured into a sentiment of, "Oh, I guess now she's trying to take over the music ministry!"

Even though my husband and I were always devoted to the pastor and his vision for the church, the rumblings that were being perpetuated throughout the congregation took on a life of their own, and we never could have imagined the divisive path that was ahead of us.

We had about six months of success at the church before things started to go south. Around January of 1997, more overt signs of conflict appeared, and rumors began swirling.

"You and your husband are going to be let go," anonymous whispers would find their way to our ears as we tried to get a better sense of the undercurrent of change that was happening. In order to regain control of the congregation, we heard that the senior pastor was considering appointing his brother as my husband's replacement.

Then there were weeks when my husband's wages would be paid late, or never show up at all, and the only explanation we'd receive was, "Oh, we'll mail that check to you soon." The rapid change in the environment was confusing and heartbreaking. It was hard to process that we'd worn out our welcome in such a short time and that our honeymoon phase at the church had abruptly concluded. After all, the pastor himself initiated the quiet campaign to usher us into leadership with buy-in from the congregation. But there was nothing quiet about what was happening now. The conflict became full-blown and vicious.

Publicly, the pastor made comments like, "I don't know what y'all are thinking, but Randolph is not the pastor; I am," he'd say, reminding the congregation who was really in charge. "I brought them here!"

In private, heated conversations between my husband and the pastor were occurring more frequently. The pastor informed us that he had decided to let us go, and allow his brother to take over the church.

I was content to give up the leadership role and return to Midland, but my husband was not. He was ready to fight. I recall one intense exchange between the pastor and my husband.

"Pastor, the people want us, not your brother" my husband argued. "Yes, you did indeed bring us here. My wife and I are newlyweds, we uprooted to relocate here, and we are ready to serve."

Knowing his influence over the people and wanting to resolve the conflict decisively, the pastor made a proposal. "Fine, let's put it to a vote. If you all win the vote, then so be it. I'll step aside and support your ministry. But if my brother wins the vote, then so be it. He will become the site pastor and take over all your duties."

So, a fight ensued. Battle lines were drawn, and everyone was forced to choose a side.

My husband and I were the new kids on the block. There was no realistic scenario in which we would have gained more favor in the congregation in six months than the pastor who they absolutely loved and who had spent years in ministry there. Although many church members had unofficially expressed their desire for us to lead them (instead of the pastor's brother), we agreed to a formal church proceeding to resolve the dispute, and a full-fledged campaign for votes commenced.

Members of the church occasionally invited us to their homes – and sometimes we hosted them in ours – and we sought to understand their feelings on the state of the church leadership. After sharing a meal and discussing light conversation topics, we'd dive into the most pressing issues.

"What do you think we should do?" my husband asked the church members as we sat around the dinner table. "My wife and I are here all the time. We don't travel to different cities or have to split our time and attention with other congregations. If it came down to a choice between us or the pastor's brother, would you have a preference?"

Dinner meetings turned into planning meetings where church members began pledging their loyalty.

"We love our senior pastor, but it's hard to see him as our leader when he's only here once a month. We love the two of you and can envision you being the pastors here. If you choose to pursue this ministry, then we are with you! We will definitely vote for you!"

The pastor made calls of his own, expressing his wishes for the congregation to abandon its fellowship with my husband and me, and vote for his brother. The pastor's message was clear and simple, "If you vote for Randolph, then you are voting against me."

The church became bitterly divided. Some of the members who had worshiped at the church for years disagreed with the way we were treated, but they loved their pastor and weren't ready to go against him. I wish we all could have found a way to push aside our human flaws and conflict and come together to carry out the church's ultimate mission of saving souls. But unfortunately, this conflict would not end amicably.

We were at the church a little over a year when the vote occurred to determine our future in the church's leadership.

I had a feeling I knew how things would turn out. Being a part of the church all my life and being aware of church politics, this scene was all too familiar.

My husband and I arrived at the church meeting where the vote would take place. The entire congregation was assembled in the sanctuary, and it felt as though we were being placed in guillotines with our fate in the hands of a throng of surrounding spectators.

I felt my husband was overly optimistic and had placed his confidence in the word of those who promised their support during the many calls or meetings in our home that had taken place in the weeks leading up to the vote.

"We have your back."

"We're going to stand up against him."

"You can count on us, Randolph."

But I don't think he had fully grasped the magnitude of what we were asking of the church members. We essentially were requesting that they break rank, realign their allegiances, and place their trust in us. I've observed pastors and church leaders since childhood, and I understand the dynamics of loyalty that can develop – sometimes even to the point of unrighteousness and dysfunction. Don't get me wrong, I have nothing against loyalty. But there should never be a question of being true to man over God. There should never be confusion or ambiguity about choosing the side of man over choosing what is right.

I was all too aware of the heavy influence of a pastor, and just because people said, "I'm with you," didn't make it so. I knew in my spirit that things were not going to end well for us that day.

As the pastor approached the podium, he proceeded to lay out his case.

"You all know why we're here today," he began. "It is my desire for my brother to take over as pastor at the church. I brought Brother Randolph here not knowing that he would betray me and try to pull you all to himself. That's not God. But because I am a man of God, I want to hear the people. So that is why we're having this vote today. By all means, if you all do not want my brother, then we will step aside."

My husband and the pastor's brother sat in the front of the sanctuary; one on the right side and the other on the left. One by one, each adult member of the congregation cast a vote into a ballot box. The extent of division about who would lead the church was on full display with some husbands' votes varying from their wives, and long-time friends choosing opposing sides.

The vote was quick and decisive, and my intuition was confirmed. After a final tally of votes, it was settled. The pastor's brother won. My husband and I lost.

Half of the crowd erupted in cheers and taunts. They clapped loudly as they shouted, "That's right! Get out! Uh huh, we told y'all to get on the winning team!" Others in the congregation who supported us sat solemnly, and some protested with a loud "boooooo!"

Some people left without speaking to each other, while others struck an accusatory tone. "You voted with them? How could you?!" There were people who had *promised* they were voting for my husband and me. We watched them do the exact opposite, and then turn to us and say, "I'm sorry. I just couldn't do it." Others looked at me as they walked down the aisle and quietly mouthed the words, "I'm sorry."

My husband quietly gathered his belongings and walked out.

It was a complete crazy mess and was one of the ugliest situations I had ever been involved in. It stung even worse because it occurred among church people. This moment reminded me that the church is a perfect institution that is filled with imperfect people. As much as we strive every day to be righteous and walk in God's will, sometimes we get it wrong. There were many people hurting that day, including me. Although I sensed an unfavorable outcome might occur, I was still in disbelief. I felt betrayed. I thought the members of the church would honor their word and stand by us. But I should have known that I was probably asking too much. Why should they choose my husband and me – who had ministered with them for mere months – over their pastor who had shepherded them for years?

Nonetheless, I was crushed, and I started crying.

That's when I heard the voices of two amazing ladies who were sitting beside me; Veronica and Ruby. These two women remind me of my mother, always beautifully dressed, well-spoken, and very ladylike. To this day, I call them my divas.

"Hold your head up," they said. "Wipe your face and walk proudly out of this building. We are right here beside you."

These ladies, along with other members of my village, stood by me through the entire process of being voted out of church leadership. I learned an invaluable lesson that day that even when everyone else turns their back, real friends in difficult times will make their allegiance known.

Immediately following the vote, the pastor's brother took over in a leadership role and my husband and I became simply… members. There were numerous people expressing the sentiment, "surely *he* is not going to lead us," but the pastor preferred his brother – who I felt was not equipped for the job. He had miscalculated the strong love for us that would develop so quickly, and what he thought he wanted (the congregation to embrace us) didn't really match his desire to maintain control of the church.

After being voted out of leadership, I had a choice to stay at home, find somewhere else to worship, or just keep going to the same church. I'm a church girl, so I couldn't just stay home. I chose to keep attending the church as a member.

"I'm going back there," I decided. "I go to worship God, so that's just what I am going to do."

My husband resumed his extensive travel to evangelize and would be away from home for weeks at a time. Consequently, I'd be left alone – again – to deal with the fallout. If it were not for my divas who stayed by my side, I couldn't have made it. They picked me up for church each week, sat with me throughout the service, and often blessed me with uplifting words. "You have nothing to hold your head down about. Hold your head up. You know who, and whose you are, and don't ever forget that."

Not surprisingly, the church's division was not resolved after the vote. On the contrary, it was amplified. There were some people who had sided with *us*, and others sided with *them*. A holy place that should be home to peace and righteousness had become a cold and hostile house where people on both sides were wounded. Church members would literally pass by one another and not speak. And some would even laugh at me.

It became very uncomfortable, and feelings of extreme anxiety and stress began to emerge. *I'm sitting in a church where I am literally not wanted, after being courted, pursued and brought here only one short year ago. How could this happen? I battled within myself. Was it my fault?*

I couldn't help but feel partially culpable for the divisive environment that resulted from the vote to remove us from leadership. Members who had been at that church for decades made a choice to befriend us – people who were very new in the city having been here a little over a year. They were now ostracized from their church home. My husband and I felt a duty to do right by them. We felt a new pressure of, *What are we all going to do now? Are we going to stay here in this unfriendly environment? Are we going to start our own church?*

It all became very heavy, knowing we had to do something, but we didn't quite know what to do. I was sleeping only three or four hours at night, constantly worrying, and still trying to paint a picture for my parents that everything was great in Chattanooga. I felt stuck in the midst of everything; I had to hear my husband complain, I had to figure out how to move forward with our new group of loyal followers at church, we were experiencing financial strains, and my home was lonely and unpeaceful.

It chipped away at me more than I knew. It was more than what my brain could process; more than what my heart could handle. I went from being frustrated and embarrassed to angry and borderline bitter. It was just too much, and I couldn't fix it.

When Betrayal Happens
Live Anyway
Practice Forgiveness

- **Forgive Even When You Don't Want To.** If you refuse to forgive, it will harm you more than those against whom you're holding a grudge. You don't want resentment and bitterness to keep you from heaven. The power of unforgiveness will sabotage the blessings that are in store for you. Go to God in prayer and ask Him for the strength to forgive.

- **Say The Words Out Loud.** Forgive out loud as if you've been asked for forgiveness. Make the choice in your heart and say the words out of your mouth; "I forgive you." Write them down. Don't speak in general terms, forgive for specific offenses. See people who hurt you for more than just one incident. Remember the times when they kept their word and were kind to you.

- **Throw A Private Forgiveness Party.** Sometimes we need a physical release of the toxic energy that is inside us. Cry, scream, throw pillows all while saying, "I forgive you!" Channel that raw energy into activities that will not bring harm to others like slashing tires or seeking revenge.

- **Change Your Vantage Point.** Try to see painful situations from the other person's point of view. Many times we are blinded by our own rage and wounds that we are unable to see that our rival is hurting, too. We are all susceptible to being consumed by our emotions and tossing our better judgment out of the window. Do not react rashly and succumb to your immediate feelings; instead allow time for cooler heads to prevail.

- **Choose Love Over Hate.** There will undoubtedly be moments that we battle with hatred and unforgiveness. Acknowledge when you've been hurt, but refuse to allow bitterness to settle in. Give yourself time for love to develop. Understand that the new position from which you choose to love may be from a different, more guarded place with a new set of rules designed to protect your heart.

SCRIPTURE AND PRAYER

For if you forgive others their trespasses, your heavenly Father will also forgive you.

Matthew 6:14

And whenever you stand praying, if you have anything against anyone, forgive him, that your Father in heaven may also forgive you your trespasses. But if you do not forgive, neither will your Father in heaven forgive your trespasses.

Mark 11:25-26 NKJV

Dear God,

Thank You for the gift of forgiveness. First of all, You forgave me. And now, I can extend that gift to others. Forgive me for my hateful thoughts, unrighteous actions, and for a judgmental spirit. There were times when I felt I deserved forgiveness, but others did not. One sin is no different from the next, and no one action is less worthy of forgiveness.

Help me to never fall into a place of self-righteousness. Help me to demonstrate unconditional love today, even to those who hurt me. I realize that my emotions do not have to control my actions. Help me to reject thoughts and emotions that are not Christ-like and only dwell on thoughts that are conducive to where You are leading me. Even if I am sad or frustrated, please let me choose to focus on positive things and not let negativity rule my emotions.

Father, may Your Word saturate my mind and direct my thoughts. Help me to release the hurt and love others the same way You love me. Amen.

3

When Exhaustion Happens
Perform Self-Care

Being relieved from our pastoral duties at the church was a huge blow to our income. When we were voted out of leadership, the $3,000 monthly checks we had been receiving for my husband's ministry stopped immediately. There was no weaning off; we instantly went from making a comfortable living to struggling to make ends meet.

Although I had secured a job at the middle school, it was the hardest – and frankly the worst – teaching position I'd ever had in my life. But I had to have it. I had to push aside my disappointment from being refused the assistant principal job and focus on what was imminent and important: eating and paying rent. Fighting for justice and retribution for the job I'd been promised wasn't going to pay Electric Power Board to keep the lights on at our apartment. Instead, I worked two jobs; I was a teacher by day and a retail salesperson by night.

My job at the middle school was a special education position working with children who had been diagnosed as emotionally disturbed. At the time, special education teaching positions were considered second class and a step down from general education positions, and they were primarily filled by African Americans. But I was optimistic because I already had experience as a bilingual teacher, a special education teacher, and general education teacher in Texas; I felt equipped to handle the challenge. What was considered undesirable by others was right up my alley. *I'm cool*, I thought to myself. *These are my babies!*

Little did I know the extent of the dysfunction I would face when trying to teach these children.

"There are about 10 students in the emotionally disturbed class," my new principal explained on my first day. "Last year they tried to set the building on fire, but you're going to do a great job helping these kids."

Most of our classes were held in portable trailers in the back of the school because my students weren't always allowed to interact in the regular education population. I arrived at work dressed in a full suit, stockings and low-heeled pumps with cute straps around my ankles.

The students gave me a very direct orientation on my first day. "This is how this class works; you let us smoke or do whatever we want," they informed me. "You just come and collect your check." I was stunned but for the most part I dismissed this brazen talk. No way were these adolescents capable of such unspeakable behavior. How bad could 6th, 7th and 8th graders really be?

They managed to answer that question without much delay. Within the first week, they kicked over desks – and kicked me in the process – they climbed out of the portable window, and sat in the back of the classroom smoking. After each incident, I set the desks upright, restrained them from climbing out of the window, stopped them from smoking, and tussled with the children in attempts to keep order.

Many other adventures took place that school year. On one occasion, a student punched me square in the face and gave me a black eye. On another occasion, one of my students snuck out of the classroom, stole a faculty member's car and backed into my brand-new red BMW.

By the time those kids finished with me, I was arriving to work every day in denim skirts, tennis shoes, hair pulled back in a ponytail and an exhausted spirit. They broke me down. My job was becoming emotionally and physically draining, but I refused to give up on them.

"What is wrong with you," they asked me angrily? "Everyone else just leaves us, but you keep coming back!" They were mad because I wanted them to learn. These kids were giving me permission to be mediocre, but I refused to accept their offer. I knew better was in them. I knew better was in me.

Even though my loyalty and compassion for people had always been one of my most redeeming qualities, it began to feel like one of the heaviest burdens to bear.

During this time of uncertainty with my husband's employment, I picked up a part-time job to help stabilize our income. After an exhausting day at school from 7 a.m. to 2 p.m., I made my way every evening from 3:30 p.m. to 9:30 p.m. to the women's department of Proffitt's, a retail store at the mall. I started out cleaning fitting rooms and eventually worked the cash registers. If my husband had taken our car out of town to evangelize, I had to figure out my transportation. Sometimes I rented a car; other times my peers from school would drop me off at work; and sometimes I took a taxi. I tried coordinating my schedule around my friends' availability so I could possibly catch a ride. But there were many nights when I was still waiting around for someone to pick me up two hours after the mall closed.

I've always had a drive for perfection. That drive kept me going nonstop, working around the clock. Growing up, I was everybody's "Little Sherry." *Little Sherry is so sweet. Little Sherry is homecoming queen, she makes good grades, and everyone loves her.* I never had a lot of room for error or failure, and I didn't allow myself the luxury of making the mistakes I needed to make.

So, on top of the drama and disappointment I was experiencing in my personal life, my career was becoming overwhelming. Being removed from our church leadership, working a 13-hour day and slowly starting to acknowledge the cracks that were forming in the foundation of my marriage all became too much. This self-imposed pressure to be flawless and be all things to all people eventually took a toll on me. One day, my body wouldn't let me go any further.

At age 28, I had a stroke.

My husband left home early one morning to work out at the gym. I wanted to have his favorite breakfast ready when he returned, so I got out of bed and made my way to the kitchen to cook. I reached into the cabinet and pulled out a plastic cup, and it dropped out of my hand.

As I reached for the salt and pepper for the eggs, I felt a strange tingling in my arm. Then, when I tried to pour milk into a bowl, my arm fell limp, my face started drooping, and my speech slurred while I tried to sing my favorite gospel hymn.

I think I'm having a stroke, I thought.

I was home alone. At this point in my marriage, I was by myself 80 percent of the time. When my husband wasn't traveling to evangelize, he was hanging out with friends or just otherwise not home. So, I called him.

"I don't feel good," I said over the phone.

"Speak up, I can't hear you," my husband said as he was at the gym, mid-workout.

"I think I'm having a stroke!"

"What?! I'll be right there," he said as he sounded very alarmed. He raced home and tried to settle me down.

I initially brushed it off thinking I'd be okay.

"Just lay on the couch, I think maybe you'll be alright," he said.

After about an hour, I said to myself, something is not right.

"I don't think I'm alright. Let's get to the hospital."

After being examined in the emergency room, it was determined I'd experienced a mild stroke.

"It's good you got to the ER when you did," the doctor explained. "It would have been much worse had you waited." He went on to detail how permanent paralysis was common for untreated stroke patients.

This was a jarring wake-up call for my husband and me, and our responses were extreme.

My husband – the only one who knew I'd had a stroke – isolated me from everyone. He didn't allow anyone to visit me. Consequently, people at the church – which we were in the process of leaving – thought I had a nervous breakdown. In my husband's mind, anything that didn't look perfect needed to be hidden. We were to maintain a picture of strength, no matter what happened.

Instead of taking any responsibility for his role in the stress I was suffering, he blamed it all on the church and lashed out at them. In reality, his always being gone and I didn't know where he was, and my working two jobs to fill the financial gaps caused more stress than anything else. All the while, I struggled to maintain the image that everything in our household was great.

After the stroke, I didn't leave my house for two weeks. This was my first encounter with depression. I was slightly ashamed of being ill and believed my physical condition would cause me to be perceived as being weak. My husband would say things like, "Strong people don't get themselves into things like this. This is a sign of weakness. You've just allowed too many people to get in your head and knock you off kilter." I would realize later that this line of thinking was his attempt at dealing with his own demons and he was projecting his insecurities onto me.

In reality, that was craziness! It was stress, not weakness!

During those two weeks at home, I tried to be still and do nothing but rest and pray. However, it was difficult for me to embrace rest. I was very anxious to get back to work because I had been this "perfect" super woman for so long. *I don't have time for this!* I thought. I refused physical therapy despite the advice of medical professionals. My stress was compounded by not being able to let go of the guilt I felt for being "weak," and I repeatedly declined the help that was offered to get me through this debilitating condition.

My doctors tried to get me to open up. "Your blood pressure is through the roof, and you truly are in a danger zone. What's going on in your life to cause this level of stress?"

In my pride, I guarded myself from exposing that I was actually falling apart physically and mentally. The only words I could seem to find were, "Nothing. I'm fine."

I now know that was foolish, but I was reverting back to my normal go-to attitude. *Let me just rebuke that. You're not going to speak negativity over my life. I am great.*

I don't advise anyone to do what I did. Mine is a miracle testimony, but it was also stupidity. It was very dangerous and could have negatively affected my entire life. I needed therapy. I needed counseling. I needed to be able to deal with my issues – from trying to be perfect to not totally dealing with the rejection I felt from Chattanooga City Schools and people telling me I'm not enough.

Even today, I sometimes push myself so far to my physical limits, that my family and friends are near tears when they warn me, "You don't understand how your health is in serious jeopardy."

God has given me the inner strength throughout my life to fight through illness, and He gives me the boldness to say with confidence, "I really am good. I am okay!" But there comes a point when even the most faithful believers need rest because an unattended need for rest leads to exhaustion. Emotional stress that is mismanaged always physically manifests itself and can cause illness.

Like the old saying goes, "God blesses babies and fools." I have behaved foolishly and recklessly in regard to safeguarding my mental and physical health. If I had to do it all over again, I would have shouted to the doctors, therapist, family and friends, "My life is crazy. I need help. If I don't get it, then I'ma lose my mind!"

Mental and physical self-care are critical for survival. For the majority of my life, self-care was not a priority for me. Quite frankly, the church didn't necessarily teach me self-care; on the contrary, it taught me more about self-sacrifice! I learned the following lessons the hard way. I wish I would have learned them sooner because I would go on to struggle with this for many years.

When Exhaustion Happens
Live Anyway
Perform Self-Care

- **Take Time For Yourself.** Take one day a week for yourself. I know that may be hard – especially if you work a full-time job. An hour a day or the first 30 minutes of every day is also sufficient, as long as you block off time that belongs to only you. Take time to focus on positive things and mentally "take out the trash." If there's any negativity that's managed to make it from the previous night to this day, then dispose of it. Use quiet time in devotion to God to recharge your battery.

- **Make Rest A Priority.** In I Kings 19:1-8, Elijah had a mountaintop experience where God told him to go eat and take a nap. His physical exhaustion was contributing to his emotional weakness to the point that he asked God to take his life. Although Elijah had just achieved victory in an armed battle, he was suddenly spooked by a far less opponent and fled to the wilderness in fear. God's angel came to Elijah and reminded him that he had great things ahead of him, and it was important to replenish before his next journey.

Elijah's story reminds us that sometimes we have to stop and replenish. We can't constantly go from one great feat to the next and not rest. When we are depleted, it changes our perspective and we are unable to see or think clearly.

- **Nourish Your Body.** When difficult things hit your life, don't refrain from eating. Exercise, get adequate sleep, keep your doctor appointments, listen to your body and stop when it's had enough. Know when you can't go any further, push any harder or last any longer. Many people in leadership, parents and others feel they have to be all things to all people. Don't feel the need to be a people pleaser. No one can be there for everyone all the time. Nobody should ALWAYS be available. The Bible tells us we are to feed and serve others from our overflow, but we can't give if our own tanks are empty. In order to give others our undivided attention, there are some days we need to give ourselves undivided attention.

- **Nourish Your Mind.** God has given us this amazing thing called the mind. If we let the mind flourish in its full potential, then it will help us think our way out of many situations. However, when the mind is tired, it can't operate at its maximum. When your mind is rested, there is a strategic process that will start in your head and you'll hear yourself say things like, *I never thought of that*. So a man thinketh, so is he. God has given us everything we need to handle every situation we go through and if we waste it on complaining and processing negative thoughts, then we will never maximize the tools that are given to us. Don't believe that any situation has to be hopeless. You can think your way out of anything, just stop and take a minute. Take some time to operate from a healthy mind. When you retreat, you can come back stronger and focused.

SCRIPTURE AND PRAYER

And he said to them, 'Come away by yourselves to a desolate place and rest a while.' For many were coming and going, and they had no leisure even to eat.

Mark 6:31

Come to me, all who labor and are heavy laden, and I will give you rest.

Matthew 11:28

Dear God,

Thank You for the example of Elijah who You fed by the brook, gave water to drink and encouraged to take a nap. I now understand that a warrior can become a worrier if he doesn't rest. Teach me to follow Your lead of taking time to rest; You are all powerful, yet You rested on the seventh day.

Forgive me for misjudging self-care for laziness and selfishness. Let me never be satisfied with feeding people from fumes. Help me to understand that if I serve people from a cup half full, it's not as good as serving from a full cup. I pray that You will anoint me with strength and courage for self-care. Help me to understand that it is not selfish to take time to secure my own physical and mental health. I pray for grace, patience and wisdom to understand that self-care is not a luxury, it is a necessity.

Release me from the guilt of taking a break to take care of myself. Help me to understand that self-care is self-love, and if I can't love myself, then I can't love my neighbor. Amen.

4

When Success Happens
Stay Humble And Focus On God

We worshipped at the same church for about three months after being voted out of leadership, but the environment simply became too hostile to continue. We were at a crossroads and had to pursue another direction.

"Maybe God brought us here to Chattanooga to start a ministry, and not assume a ministry," my husband said.

His words struck a chord within me and awakened a spirit that I hadn't allowed to flourish in a long time. His unwillingness to be defeated ignited the fight in me, and I immediately jumped on board. Although I had only rested for two weeks after my mild stroke, I pressed my internal "Go" button. I felt it was time to get back to business; we pushed forward, full steam ahead and didn't slow down. So, in the fall of 1997, we gave birth to a new church and founded Living Word Ministries.

"A Living Word for a dying world," my husband declared. "That's our motto!"

A small group of friends, fellow ministers and about 20 people who also left our previous congregation joined us on our adventure and walked with us on the journey to give birth to Living Word Ministries. Until we found a permanent home, we held worship services from place to place for about a year. We first started meeting in the clubhouse of the apartment complex where my husband and I lived. We also utilized Boys and Girls Clubs, funeral home chapels or any venue that would accommodate us during our infancy phase.

Every Saturday, the members and I prepared for Sunday services a day in advance. We'd set up rented audio equipment – one member configured the speakers while another adjusted the microphones. We set up 50 chairs – always optimistic we'd have multiple visitors – and each person invited a friend or two to services the next day. Without the contributions from each person during these beginning moments, the church's success would not have been conceivable. I'm a firm believer that we do not succeed alone, and there are always others who help make our individual and collective success possible.

"Thank you all so much for coming," I greeted the audience at the beginning of every service. "We are so excited to have you. We're a new ministry, and we believe this is what God has called us to do. We promise if you join us while we follow God, then you will not regret it."

After a few short announcements, I'd lead the congregation in praise and worship. Many of the people who attended our new church were singers, and our newly-minted minister of music could make two or three singers sound like a beautiful ensemble. From the onset, Living Word had an amazing music ministry, an energetic husband and wife duo to pastor the church, and talented members with unmatched optimism and enthusiasm.

My husband would preach, we'd all pray, and two hours later we'd all pitch in to break down and transform whatever venue we were in back to its original form.

"See you again next Sunday! Everyone, invite a friend next week. We're going to grow this ministry one person at a time."

I knew starting a new church was going to be very hard. We knew there would be weeks and days that didn't go as planned.

For example, there were several times when we conducted church in parking lots because the venue in which we were planning to worship was unexpectedly unavailable. On one occasion, we found ourselves locked out of the community center where we held Sunday service because the building manager failed to meet us there to unlock the building, nor did he leave us the key so we could let ourselves in.

With nearly 30 families en route to gather with us, we had to think fast. We scrambled to find any solution that would gain us access inside the building. We frantically checked around the perimeter, hoping to find an unlocked door or window. But, no such luck.

Standing on a concrete lot in the middle of a Tennessee summer is quite unpleasant, but we did our best to put a positive spin on it. As attendees began arriving and noticing that we were congregated outside, we encouraged them to stay.

"Unfortunately, today we are locked out of the building, but aren't you glad that Jesus never locks us out?! Hallelujah!"

"If we have church in the parking lot, it gives the community an opportunity to hear God's word, and join us in worship!"

"This way, you don't even have a ceiling interrupting your praise to God; it'll go directly to heaven. Isn't that cool?!"

The music ministry performed acapella that day, and my husband preached without a microphone and speakers. Because there were not enough chairs for everyone, some people had to stand. So, we shortened the sermon and did our best to make the service conducive for the circumstances.

"For those of you who have the joy of the Lord in your legs, this is going to be a standing service! Hang in here with us for this service, you will not regret being here with us today."

There were some people who didn't buy into our proposal. When they arrived and realized that it was an outdoor service, they immediately got back into their vehicles and went elsewhere. But those who chose to stay witnessed that we wouldn't give up and we would do whatever it took to keep moving forward. We could have just canceled the service, shut everything down and walked away, but we didn't.

When you're leading people, they want to see how you respond in a crisis and if they'll be able to count on you. That type of leadership goes beyond charisma and people simply liking you; it tests your substance, stick-to-it-ness and sustainability. If people can see your vision for the future, then it makes it easier to stand with you in the present.

Regardless of the challenges, pastoring Living Word was what my husband and I believed we should do. Starting a new church wasn't foreign to me. I had watched my mother and father do it when I was a child. My father founded a church in Midland, Texas, in a small building with a few parishioners from his previous congregation, and together they built a ministry that has lasted for decades.

Even though my siblings and I were barely toddlers when my parents moved to Midland for ministry work, I remember the challenges of starting a ministry. Week after week, we were in church learning how to sing, usher, speak publicly and serve, all while watching my father lead. There were countless meetings, prayer and consecration times, conferences and pastoral duties that required my parents' complete devotion and self-sacrifice. They labored tirelessly every day, contributing large portions of their personal finances to the church and teaching their children, by example, how to work hard and passionately pursue their callings. I remember witnessing all of my parents' hard work, and I also remember the fruit of it; watching people's lives transform became a common occurrence. People were coming off the street and accepting Jesus as Lord and Savior of their lives.

This new opportunity with my husband was history repeating itself. I was a product of my environment. I wanted to be like my mom who was an amazing church administrator who faithfully supported my dad's ministry. Although there were stark differences in how my husband and my dad operated, I always knew my destiny was to be a helpmate to my husband. I took my role as supporting my husband very seriously, and I was ready to use all of my gifts and my talents to propel him forward. I was a natural born worker and his biggest cheerleader. When we decided to start our ministry, I assumed the role of rallying the people. "You want people to come? I can gather the masses!" I assured him. "We're going to do this! Don't worry, honey. We're going to be good."

After a year of our church worshipping in temporary locations, in 1998, we purchased a 16,500 square foot property in the heart of the city where we built our ministry for over a decade. The building itself was 100 years old, was on the National Register of Historic Places and was a fixer-upper that required a lot of work. Nonetheless, we were excited to have a place to call our own. The days leading up to our first service, we made extensive repairs, painted, and cleaned for hours to make our new location an inviting home.

Our new church building was located a short, five-minute walk away from the University of Tennessee at Chattanooga, so we were on campus regularly inviting students to join us. We canvassed the area with Saturday morning door-knocking efforts that would rival any elected official campaign today.

"Good morning!" we cheerfully greeted everyone who

graciously answered their doors. "We're a new church in the area, and we would love for you to join us for worship tomorrow morning, or for one of our other services during the week." We distributed flyers around the neighborhood, broadcasted public service announcements at local TV and radio stations, hosted neighborhood picnics and other community outreach activities to spread the word.

We poured every ounce of ourselves into our burgeoning ministry, leveraging a lifetime of exposure to cutting edge spiritual leaders who had shown us the "building from the ground up" model. My husband had traveled with international speakers and learned how they moved crowds with beautifully crafted oratorical messages. And the parenting I received from two dedicated servants of God defined my world view and perspective on kingdom building from an early age.

Our work began to pay off. God provided an amazing increase as the Living Word membership grew from 20 members to over 400 within five years. Familiar faces from our previous congregation as well as new people from around the city began filling our pews each week. In the early 2000s in our geographical region, that was huge! Our college ministry was wildly successful, our choir and music department were second to none. We began hosting monthly college nights and an annual, three-day ministry event called The Joshua Generation Conference. We flew nationally-known speakers to Chattanooga for the conference and hundreds of attendees from across the region packed our building to the max. The overflow of people was left standing around the wall. Living Word developed a reputation as the fresh fragrance Chattanooga had been waiting on. As "outsiders" from another state, we didn't necessarily follow the status quo, and we continuously brought new, unconventional – even radical – ideas to the table. My husband made me a co-pastor when female pastors were taboo in the denomination we were a part of at the time. The roles reserved for women typically included being missionaries or evangelists – otherwise known as female preachers. As our ministry grew, I became the energetic spark that could lead praise and worship, and preach!

At the same time, my husband and I were emerging as Chattanooga's darling, powerhouse couple. We were both educated with masters degrees – mine in educational leadership and his in theology – which was not prevalent in our denomination at that time. Our ministry was unique in that we were a dual talent; we could both sing, exhort and connect with our followers on a deep level. We also became materially blessed; we were able to own properties around the city, drive nice cars and wear nice clothes. While our church grew, our family grew; my husband and I were blessed with two beautiful children – a girl and a boy. I also had a career that was taking off and propelling me to a different kind of notoriety in the business community. My husband continued to develop his craft as a charismatic preacher and gained popularity as he traveled to speak to audiences across the state and nationally.

"You all have the ability to take over this city," we were told by other pastors in the area. "We don't know how y'all are doing this, but the way people are drawn to you is powerful!"

Becoming a new hot commodity in the city was unexpected, but we knew starting a church and having followers came with great responsibility to the people. Growing into this new leadership role was challenging, but it was a wonderful time of using our lives to glorify God. My personal journey then became one of balancing church, motherhood, marriage and a burgeoning career.

    I believe that the definition of "success" is determined by each individual's unique goals and desires. My growth and maturation throughout life also taught me that my mission to achieve success is an ongoing journey and not the pursuit of a final destination. Above all, the manner in which I realize my dreams is more important than the praise or accolades that may accompany my achievements. There are points in everyone's career when you are presented with a choice to take shortcuts, push the ethical envelope or flat out violate the rules to get what you want. That's just the world we live in. But my prayer has always been that God keeps my heart and intentions pure as I chase my ambitions and try to make them reality.

Was I willing to work hard?
Did I maintain my integrity?
Was I a nice person to my colleagues and peers?
Did I show respect to my superiors?

    If I can answer "yes" to questions like these, then I believe I've accomplished my true goals and attained *good* success.

    Many times, the road to success is paved with obstacles that obstruct your view so drastically that it becomes hard to imagine there could be anything on the other side that's worth all the trouble. You will recall that my first year as a teacher in Chattanooga was a doozy. I loved teaching, but the children in my emotionally disturbed class challenged me every day. But, by grace and with much patience, we managed to finish the nine-month school year with several of my students being "mainstreamed" into the regular education population. Those same kids who were relegated to portable classrooms outside of the main building, who smoked in class and tried to set things on fire were able to join their peers in standard curriculum classes. That definitely became a bright spot for me, the students and the staff.

Working with the children in my emotionally disturbed middle school class was a training ground that taught me how to push through adversity. It was my boot camp that prepared me to enter and rise through the ranks of the Chattanooga school system. Little did I know that while my head was buried in my day-to-day duties and my focus was solely on putting out immediate fires each week, I was being observed from afar by people who had the power and influence to change my life.

One day during my first year as a teacher at this middle school, I went to check on my students who were in algebra class. While walking in the hallway, I observed an irate parent who had cornered our principal, Andy, in a fiery exchange. Andy's face was beet red with frustration and confusion, and the parent was not letting him get a word in edgewise. I had no idea what had caused this confrontation, but I knew right away that something had to be done to deescalate the situation. My principal and I had worked as a tag-team on many issues before, so I jumped in and tried to help.

"Hello, ma'am. I noticed you're having a little bit of difficulty," I interjected. In an attempt to lighten the mood, I jokingly said, "I know Andy can be a handful sometimes."

"And who are you?" the parent abruptly asked.

"I'm his friend," I said. "Let me see if I can help you out."

For reasons I'll never know, the parent opened up to me in that moment in a way that I did not expect. She explained all the reasons why she was upset, and I strategically walked her through solutions to all of her concerns as we stood in the school hallway. Slowly, she calmed down as each problem seemed closer to a possible resolution.

After successfully deescalating the situation, the parent asked Andy to forgive her bad behavior. Then we all hugged and conducted a brief meeting in Andy's office to address the underlying issue more thoroughly. When the meeting adjourned and the parent departed, I exhaled with a sigh of relief and took a moment to gather myself. That's when my focus shifted to a gentlemen who was also in Andy's office, but I did not know who he was.

"You need to be a school administrator," this stranger said to me.

"And... who are you?" I politely asked.

"I am Ray Swafford, the Director of Operations for Chattanooga City Schools and I'm here to change your world today."

I was completely oblivious to the fact that Mr. Swafford – my boss's boss who was responsible for more than 10 schools including mine – had been standing at the end of the hallway and witnessed my entire encounter with the disgruntled parent.

"I am shocked that I have never heard of you before, but it was a pleasure watching you work today," he said. "Mrs. Randolph, we have interviews for an assistant principal position today at 4:30 p.m. and I want you there."

Today?! Moments ago, I was headed to check on my newly transitioned students in algebra class. Now, our director wants me to attend an interview with no time to prepare?!

"I can't interview today," I argued. "I haven't prepared. What should I bring with me? I don't know what to do!"

"You know what you did out in that hallway today? Go do that," he said.

Mr. Swafford had never met me. He just liked what he saw in one incident that he observed, plus my boss vouched for me. Chattanooga City Schools and Hamilton County Schools were preparing to merge into one – the Hamilton County Department of Education – and they were hiring for multiple open positions. Less than one year after being told by the human resources representative that I "wasn't ready," I was being discovered by the person who had the hiring power and influence to actually change my life.

I hurried home, grabbed a suit and heels from the back of my closet and made my way to the interview.

"Mrs. Randolph, what makes you think you can be an administrator over a school," I was asked as I sat in front of a 17-person interview panel that included the school system superintendent, all four of the directors including Mr. Swafford, principals and other central office staff.

I wanted to point to Mr. Swafford and say, *because that man right there told me!* But I didn't reveal what prompted me to show up that day. Besides, being an assistant principal had been my original plan in the first place. I had just experienced an unexpected detour.

I answered every question as competently as I could and left the room feeling confident and eager to learn the outcome. The results came within a week. Out of 25 candidates who interviewed that day, I was the only one who received a perfect score of 17 out of 17. "Congratulations, Sheryl," Mr. Swafford commended me. "Next year, you're going to be an assistant principal at a Hamilton County School System elementary school."

In 1997, during the same time my husband and I were planting our new church Living Word Ministries, I became an assistant principal.

I owe so much of my career advancement to those with influence and generosity like Andy, Mr. Swafford, and Mrs. Swanson, my supervisor at my first assistant principal job. Even at my first position as a teacher for emotionally disturbed children, people like Coach Taylor, the girls basketball coach, and Coach Green, the boys athletic coach, saw my talents and chose to mentor, nurture and be a champion for me so that I could flourish and reach my full potential. It's important to be connected to positive and influential people. Having "the goods" isn't always sufficient. Sometimes you need someone to believe in you enough to open the door and help you walk through it.

For example, in 1999, two years after working as an assistant principal, a principal position became available at an urban school that needed some fresh, innovative, and new ideas. I wanted to apply, but this time the process would be tricky because I had a seven-month-old infant.

"I know you have what it takes," Mr. Swafford told me when I inquired about the position. "But we don't have any principals who have a baby. This work is so hard, Sheryl, I don't think you can do it with a young baby."

He was right about one thing; being a school administrator was hard work. Not to mention, I was a brand-new mother and the co-founder of a young ministry. It was a lot. Honestly, it was probably more than I should have even considered doing at one time, especially since I had pushed myself beyond my limits before to the detriment of my health. But my drive to advance and accomplish my professional goals outweighed it all. I lobbied for the job with one condition.

"I promise I can do this," I assured Mr. Swafford. "I just need you to give me some help."

He took a chance on me – again.

"Okay, Sheryl. I'll hire you for the job, but I'm going to place two assistant principals at the school to help you."

At the time, two assistant principals were never assigned to one elementary school. Mr. Swafford was breaking the mold. His strategy later became known as "the Ray Swafford model," and it was piloted at my school. My two assistant principals were as solid as rocks. One was a veteran educator named Gail Morgan who became a dear friend and one of my greatest supporters. She was a community historian who was intimately familiar with the nuances of the school's neighborhood, and she knew the families that our students came from. The other was a young curriculum specialist who was skilled at teaching struggling students how to read and at helping teachers with their professional development. I completed the trio with my soft skills that enhanced my ability to lead and manage people. The three of us were a mighty force.

We implemented strategies that were unconventional at the time in the district such as guided reading groups, after school programs, and a three-tier model where one assistant principal was focused solely on kindergarten through second graders, and the other attended only to third, fourth and fifth graders. We became better administrators. We worked tirelessly every day. There were nights when my daughter laid across my lap while I sat at the computer completing paperwork.

We conducted community outreach using many of the same tactics my husband and I employed to build our church. We rode the school bus to the neighborhoods where our students lived and walked the streets introducing ourselves.

"There is new leadership in the city," we declared when we met with parents. "We believe these kids are smart and can be successful. We are going to do it together." Our school was in the midst of public housing complexes and most of our students lived in low-income housing developments. But we were on a mission to eliminate that as an excuse. We didn't focus on their poverty, we focused on their potential. "All children will achieve. No exceptions. No excuses." That was our motto.

Together we improved a failing school's proficiency – from 12 percent to 66 percent – so quickly that we gained recognition from the state of Tennessee. Even though we were below the state's 70 percent proficient threshold to be labeled as "passing," to us, we were a Grade A school.

After five years at the principal post and also welcoming my second child, I wanted a break. It was a priceless time in my life when I wanted to bond with my newborn as well as be at home more often as my daughter entered kindergarten. My employer offered a very convenient benefit that allowed me to take a year of unpaid leave but I could return with the same seniority I had when I left.

While the hiatus was very refreshing and much needed, our family soon missed the income, insurance, and other benefits my career provided that allowed us to maintain the lifestyle we had grown accustomed to. So after working a short, part-time stint as the Vice President of Education and Health at the Urban League of Chattanooga, I returned to Hamilton County Schools in February 2006 as interim principal at an elementary school. It was a suitable position to get reacquainted with the system as well as become oriented with all the changes that had occurred since my leave of absence. And of course, it wasn't long before another opportunity arose to advance my career once again.

"The district is hiring a new Director of Student Services," Mr. Swafford informed me. "I think you should go online and apply."

This position was responsible for overseeing services such as enrollment and student transfers from one school to another for all 42,000 students in the district. This director also supervised social workers and enforced Title VI and Title IX policies that ensured equality for everyone.

I felt comfortable running a school, but the idea of the director position felt out of reach for me. Plus, there were several other qualified candidates who had doctorate degrees and no gaps in their careers at the school district. Nonetheless, I went for it. What did I have to lose? Plus, Mr. Swafford was a steady encourager and cheerleader who made me believe I could hit just about any goal I set my sight on.

"You've got this," he convinced me. "And, I'm here to support you! You will be just fine."

I applied for the position, was granted an interview and faced the selection panel with my head held high. Assistant superintendents, school directors, human resources professionals and the like peppered me with questions during the hour-long interview. When it was all over, I went home certain that the other candidates who I felt were shoo-ins for the position would outshine me by far. Yet, I was appreciative for the opportunity to take part in the process.

I had no expectations that I would get the job, so when the superintendent called after three days with an offer, I was floored.

"Are you ready to work, Mrs. Randolph?" he asked. "If you are willing, we would like to offer you the position to be Director of Student Services for Hamilton County Schools."

I was over the moon. From being a young special education teacher a few short years ago to being director; things were really starting to come together for me.

When Success Happens
Live Anyway
Stay Humble And Focus On God

- **Keep Working.** Achieving success requires lots of hard work. Maintaining that level of success requires an equal amount or even more work. Don't fall into the "I've arrived" mentality. You've never arrived. Greater opportunity calls for greater responsibility, and smarter working. Start networking and partner up with people who complement your skill set. Allow other people's talents to grow as yours do and empower others. When you learn to take your hands off of *everything*, other people can put their hands on *some* things. The greatest part about being a leader is when you develop and create other leaders.

- **Seek Heavenly Direction.** When you are responsible for leading others, it is important to look to God for guidance. Meditation and prayer should become part of your everyday routine. Pray for wisdom and direction. Many times I say, "God, if you don't lead me, then I won't know where to go." When you are treading in unfamiliar territory, you always have to go to the One who's been there and done that; and that's God. Today is new to us, but it's not new to Him. Proverbs 3:6 tells us to acknowledge Him in all our ways, and He'll direct our path. Don't allow man's plan to supersede God's plan. Be careful of becoming bigger than God and relying on yourself and not Him.

- **Maintain Your Integrity.** Joshua 1:8–9 teaches us that we should strive for "good" success. You accomplish good success by following God's commandments and doing things the right way. Never settle for ill-gotten gains. Your integrity and reputation should never be sacrificed for the sake of personal or professional advancement. That would be bad success and its rewards lack honor and sustainability.

- **Stay Humble.** It has been said throughout history that power has the potential to corrupt an individual's character. Be diligent in always treating people right, because the same people you see on the way up could be the same ones you meet on the way down. Stay humble, remain teachable and keep yourself on an even keel when success occurs. Don't let your conversation become, "look what *I* did." Stay focused on what *God* has done.

SCRIPTURE AND PRAYER

For by the grace given to me I say to everyone among you not to think of himself more highly than he ought to think, but to think with sober judgment, each according to the measure of faith that God has assigned.

Romans 12:3

Whatever you do, work heartily, as for the Lord and not for men

Colossians 3:23

Dear God,

I am grateful for the blessing of walking in my kingdom assignment. Thank You for choosing me to walk in a path of leadership and trusting that I will remain aligned with Your will and Your way. You sustained me in hard times and allowed me to see the fruit of my labor. Thank You for allowing me to arrive at my harvest with a sound mind and with my integrity intact. All my talent and abilities come from You. Help me to always walk worthy of that honor so that everything I do brings glory to You.

Forgive me for the times when I tried to rely on myself to attain success. I can do all things through Christ; help me to remember it is always "we" do it together and not just "me." Please keep me self-aware and mindful that I was never the Creator of my gifts, but the keeper and steward only. Thank You for everyone who You placed in my path who helped refine my talents, groomed and matured them, and prepared me to use them for Your good works. Amen.

5

When Duality And Doubt Happen
Know Your Worth

The role of Director of Student Services was one of the most high-profile positions I've had in my professional career. I couldn't have been more excited to be offered the job which I started in 2006, ten years after my initial arrival to Chattanooga.

I knew my education, experience and talent qualified me for the role. My previous success turning schools around and ascending the ranks from special education teacher to director boosted my confidence. Even still, being responsible for 42,000 students and supervising nearly 20 staff members was quite intimidating. Before stepping into the role, I experienced hints of inadequacy. I questioned myself.

Am I ready for this?

What if I make mistakes?

Am I equipped to play the political game that comes along with highly visible, public occupations?

Am I truly good enough?

Are there more qualified people who would do a better job than I can?

My first few months on the job did little to quell those feelings. I was challenged like never before. In addition to the natural learning curve that comes with any career shift, I faced an unexpected spirit of rebellion among personnel under my supervision. There was a palpable tension between a small group of my direct reports and me because – while I wasn't formally trained and certified in their areas of expertise – I'd been awarded a position for which they believed I was neither qualified nor prepared.

They tested me to my absolute limits. Unlike the special education middle school students who brazenly initiated me during my first days with the school system, these professionals' attacks were more calculated, more audacious and infuriating. In staff meetings, they wore headphones while I was talking and said, "let us know when you start speaking about relevant topics that we need to hear."

The boldest ones attempted to trap me with trick questions, quizzing me on fake policies that did not even exist, and publicly challenging me at every turn in hopes that I would fail.

I'm not sure what their resentment towards me was rooted in, but I knew they were hardworking, passionate people who felt overworked and overlooked. Somehow, watching me squirm appeared to bring them a sense of satisfaction, but it angered me.

I was forced to be a leader and a student at the same time. However, I had members of my team who wouldn't let me learn. It's hard leading people where you are not as skilled because they challenge what you don't know. Every day, I had to dig in and educate myself. I researched everything I didn't know. I consulted with friends outside of the school system to get answers to all my questions. I wondered if this was the job that would finally make or break me. If I couldn't conquer this, then what did that mean for the future of my career?

I always exhibited a poised and confident demeanor, but this new position was one of the first times I wavered inside. I believe everyone faces moments in life that, no matter how much greatness you've accomplished and regardless of how fortified your exterior is, doubt creeps in. I like to describe this phenomenon as living in duality. It's a common experience that happens to all of us. For example, we want to display strength at all times, even though there are moments when we feel weak. Or, we manage to be courageous while we simultaneously are afraid and anxious.

Living in duality can permeate any part of life. Some career-driven professionals believe they can't show signs of weakness on the job, even if they need help or guidance from others. Some women feel they must hide their tears or they'll be dismissed as emotional and unstable. And some men may believe confessing their fears discredits their manhood. I believe we must seek a healthy balance of strength and vulnerability. We should all strive to reconcile our public and private personas in a manner that reflects the true complexity of the human experience.

Personally, I learned a painful lesson about the danger of imbalance in this area of my life.

For many years, I was publicly happy, and my husband and I were thriving. Our careers were flourishing, we lived in a gorgeous house and every time we hit the streets, we looked like the "rich and famous." We drove Range Rovers and Mercedes and lodged at the Ritz Carlton when we traveled. Our children were dressed in the finest clothes, I was a doting wife, and we had a picture-perfect family.

However, behind closed doors, I was miserable, and our home was unraveling. My marriage became characteristic of sparkly by day, and a black hole of darkness by night. Over time, we learned to play our "roles" when we had an audience, but our private life was in constant conflict.

I vividly remember an evening in Memphis, Tennessee, where my family attended a church convention. Our daughter was only a toddler, and we were just starting to hit our stride as a power preacher duo. My husband and I were in our hotel room embroiled in one of many heated discussions that frequently plagued our marriage. I don't recall the specific catalyst for this argument, but the hallmark event was all too familiar.

"You make me sick," my husband shouted in disgust. "When this convention is over, I'm out of here. I am done!"

"You know, if that's what you want to do, then fine," I responded. "By the way, I'm not going to the evening worship in the convention center tonight. I don't feel like it. I'm going to have dinner with our daughter and simply relax."

"Oh yes, you are," he replied. "We are a family and people are expecting us. You are going to put on this dress, and we are going."

All I wanted to do that night was take a timeout and retreat from the spotlight. I didn't want to put on a charade. I was tired and didn't have the strength to pretend that everything was okay. But I knew my absence would raise questions, and at the end of the day, I decided I was the protector of our image. And that's what made me get up and go.

Getting ready for the convention hall that night felt like preparing for a live stage play. Our expensive wardrobes were costumes. My hair and makeup were flawless, and we looked fabulous from head to toe.

After getting dressed, we left the hotel room and our disdain for each other came right along with us. My husband walked several paces ahead of me down the hallway, and we gave each other the silent treatment as we made our way downstairs.

When we reached the main floor, the elevator doors opened

just like curtains parting for the opening act of a stage play. *Action!* We immediately joined hands as we entered the conference hall, plastered smiles on our faces and acted out our roles. We played our characters. We delivered a performance for the world that night that rivaled any Broadway show.

"I'd like to introduce you to my lovely wife," my husband presented me to individuals around the ballroom. "She is so wonderful."

Even though we had just finished dueling it out and trading animosities, we sat close during the worship service, like husbands and wives do, and we carried out our act; it was well-rehearsed because we had done it so many times.

In that moment, life felt fake, and I hated that feeling. I felt guilty for being inauthentic. Being happy was no longer my goal, and I just settled for the performance. I smiled through it as people showered us with constant compliments. "Y'all are such an amazing couple. I want what y'all have." When, ironically, I had become envious of other people in seemingly healthy relationships.

Our ministry, however, was not a performance. It was sincere and pure. We were able to minister to others despite our own imperfections. We were able to positively affect people's lives, even though we couldn't get ourselves together. We couldn't master our own teachings inside our home. We were unable to master talking to each other, the way we mastered helping other couples.

That night in Memphis, we went to dinner with other couples following the worship service before returning to the hotel for the evening. We unlocked the door to our room, walked inside, and the show was over. We didn't speak to each other for the rest of the night. We climbed into separate beds and turned out the lights.

In fairness, a lot of this is normal. All couples have disagreements and are forced to pause their fights until they can resume them in private. But with us, it became deeper. These occasional events became a lifestyle; and the lifestyle became toxic, unhealthy, and filled with insults and verbal attacks on my self-esteem.

For example, when I struggled with infertility early in our marriage, he said, "You can't even have a baby right. What are you good for?"

At times he rebuffed my attempts at affection saying, "If you weren't so fat, maybe I would be attracted to you. Nobody else is ever going to want you, either."

Or, one of the classic lines: "Oh, you're Mrs. Goody Two-shoes. You think you are so smart and perfect, because 'everybody loves Sherry!'"

These moments were heartbreaking, and I asked time and time again, "what have I done? What did I do wrong?"

In a matter of days or sometimes just a couple of hours, he always reversed course and asked for forgiveness. "You know I'm just playing; I don't know why I say these dumb things. You're the best thing that ever happened to me. I love you and I'm sorry. It's not you, it's me."

The emotional rollercoaster was baffling and bewildering. But most of all, it was hurtful. I never feared he would physically harm me, but he knew how to use his words very well; he didn't have to touch me to hurt me. Whoever originated the phrase "sticks and stones may break my bones, but words will never hurt me," was a brilliant manipulator. Because that is the biggest lie! Yes, words do hurt!

Emotional abuse was much more impactful than hitting me. Being neglected, isolated and constantly criticized nearly drove me crazy. It triggered self-doubt and insecurity, both which can allow one to tolerate abuse. My self-esteem and self-confidence gradually chipped away. I became a shell of myself; a strong and sturdy rock deteriorated into a pebble.

But to the rest of the world, I never let on. Through it all, I was determined to be a good wife and mother. I stood by his side at every church service, I made sure dinner was always on the table every night, the kids were cared for and I was the best homemaker I knew how to be. I thought I was strong enough and I would be fine. I never talked to anybody about this. I didn't even tell my own mother, my best friend, about it. I didn't want our image to be destroyed.

To this day, it is difficult to pinpoint why I accepted this treatment for so long. I constantly battled within. One day I would tell myself, *things will get better.* The next day, I would say to myself, *You don't have to take this! You're smart enough, you don't need him.* And the next day, *No, we have to keep the family together.*

I have to take some responsibility for what I allowed to happen to me. I believe God holds us accountable for doing our part. Somewhere along the line, I became complicit and part of the problem when I didn't address it and demand better. Instead, I began justifying the behavior.

Well, he's never laid a hand on me, so is it really abuse?

Over time, I started devaluing myself.

I guess this is what I deserve.

I stopped loving myself. My closest friends who caught glimpses of what was going on behind the scenes said, "You don't love yourself. If you did, you wouldn't allow yourself to be mistreated like this."

Those comments made me incredibly angry, but they were true. I didn't love myself enough. I started loving my husband and our public image more than I loved myself, and that is dangerous. Even the Bible says to love your neighbor as yourself. We frequently fail to properly execute this command. We start loving our neighbors above ourselves and in spite of ourselves. But He said "as." My circumstance became unhealthy because I stopped loving "as" myself and I loved "more than." It became about protecting my husband's welfare at all cost, and nothing was left over for me.

Naturally, I began questioning my judgement.

Had I made the wrong decision with my marriage?

Had I rushed into something? My whirlwind romance – that I always believed was divinely ordered – wasn't turning into my happily ever after.

Where was the man I had fallen head over heels for?

My husband and I shared happy moments, but we were not living a happy life. When I found myself having to justify moments more than celebrating moments, then I knew my life was not balanced.

As much as I tried to conceal my unhappiness, I couldn't hide forever. Eventually, our strife at home began showing itself in public, specifically at church. Comments made from the pulpit from week to week revealed the volatile and unstable nature of our marriage to our entire congregation.

One week, the power struggle between my husband and me was on full display.

"Nothing can be led by two heads. Anything that has two heads is a two-headed monster," he said as he suggested that I was trying to take over the congregation that he made me co-pastor over. "*I'm the head here. No one is going to take this ministry from me.*"

The next week, he lovingly waved to the children and me from the pulpit and sang songs of praise.

Members of our church watched every week as I sat alone on the pew, stone-faced and unresponsive to the whiplash of conflicting activities. I later learned that many people wondered how and why I accepted that behavior.

One day, a lady at church, with whom I occasionally chatted, gave me an unexpected gift.

"Sheryl, I'd like you to have this book," she said. "It's a really good read about an abused wife. But the interesting part is, she doesn't know she's being abused."

"Oh my, I feel so sorry for her," I said with sincere compassion. "That just saddens me for women who are going through that."

I continued, "I hate when men do that. That is so wrong! Women have to be strong, and sometimes, if it's not working, they have to call it quits and walk out. I know walking out is not easy, but sometimes it's the only option."

As I went through my whole women empowerment spiel, she looked at me with an incredulous expression. *Poor thing. She doesn't even know that the woman in the book is just like her.*

I "felt sorry" for other people, who were just like me. I was in their same circumstance and I couldn't even see it.

When Duality And Doubt Happen
Live Anyway
Know Your Worth

- **Reject Negativity.** Let your inner voice of affirmation be louder than any negativity that is being said on the outside. For every criticism, give yourself two compliments and outweigh unconstructiveness. Only digest things that are edifying. You can't stop the world from talking, but you can stop digesting what is unhelpful. Don't waste energy worrying about what others think of you. Never justify abuse or tell yourself it is okay to be devalued and mistreated.

- **Find Power In Positive Words.** Say affirmations out loud and don't just think them in your heart. "I am unique." "I am amazing." "I am the righteousness of God." Practice saying these things out loud. The Bible speaks about the power of words. Be intentional about putting positive words in your atmosphere. God had the power to say, "let there be" and there was. If He is inside of us, then we have that same power. Fast from harmful and destructive words and speak only the things that the Bible tells us in Philippians 4:8 to meditate on; things that are true, honest, just, pure, lovely and commendable. Let that be your criteria. If it does not fit in *those* things, don't let it come out of your mouth.

- **Be True To Your Authentic Self.** Don't try to be what other people want you to be, and never live for other people's approval instead of your own happiness. Accept that much of your life will be lived in duality. You will always be stronger in some areas of life than in others. Release the guilt of feeling that you have to be strong all the time or be good at everything. Strong and weak can go together. Just because you need strengthening in one area does not mean you are not strong. Simply make sure the area in your life that needs improvement gets the attention it requires. Don't settle for your life being a performance. Live passionately and achieve the life you actually want.

- **Focus On Your Purpose And Value.** If you're thinking you have no purpose, remember that we are all here for a reason. God has amazing plans for you, so be intentional about living your life. Getting you to think you are not good enough is one of the Enemy's weapons of deception. He knows if you discover who you really are, you will be unstoppable. When in doubt, focus on things that you do well. Put yourself in places where good things are happening and being said. Turn your attention to what is working right. Those things have a way of validating you.

SCRIPTURE AND PRAYER

For the one who doubts is like a wave of the sea that is driven and tossed by the wind. For that person must not suppose that he will receive anything from the Lord; he is a double-minded man, unstable in all his ways.

James 1:6-8

Do not be conformed to this world, but be transformed by the renewal of your mind, that by testing you may discern what is the will of God, what is good and acceptable and perfect.

Romans 12:2

Dear God,

Thank You for Your grace during my times of double-mindedness. Only You can restore my mind to a place of soberness and peace. Thank You for reminding me of my value. Help me to never forget that You knitted me together in my mother's womb, and I am worthy because You created me and You love me. Help me to know I am worth being celebrated and not just tolerated.

Please forgive me when I do not live according to Your image. When I trade Your image for man's, then I forfeit my privilege and accept limitations on my life. Transform my mind so that I will not be conditioned by the fantasies of this world. Help me to live in reality and grant me the courage to never present an inauthentic version of myself to the world.

Teach me to find my identity and know who I am. Fortify my discernment and let me never settle for anything less than my destiny. Amen.

6

When Loss Happens
Accept What God Allows

"Sheryl, the doctors think your mom may have had a mild stroke," my dad informed me on a fateful day in March 2008. "They're going to keep a close eye on her and monitor her condition for the next few weeks."

"What? How is this possible?" I asked in complete shock. "Just a month ago, she received the best health report she's had in years! She's been exercising, her blood pressure and cholesterol are down, she's lost weight. She was doing everything right."

"It caught us all off guard," he agreed. "But she has been experiencing slight paralysis in her right arm and can't get a grip on things. We first noticed when she dropped a cup in the kitchen."

That specific symptom was eerily familiar, and I stopped in my tracks when I heard it. Eleven years prior to that moment, my stroke symptoms manifested themselves in the exact same way; dropping items in the kitchen while trying to cook breakfast. While it was terrifying to hear this diagnosis about my mother, I took some comfort in knowing if I could make a full recovery from the same incident, then surely, with prayer and healing from God, so could she.

For months, my mother continued to display unexplained weakness in her hands, arms, feet and legs, so my sister, Sharnette, moved back to Midland in the fall of 2008 to help care for her. After countless medical tests and a thorough process of elimination, the doctors ruled out a stroke but could not definitively identify the cause of her symptoms. It wasn't until she visited a specialist that we got accurate answers.

With tears in his eyes, a young physician delivered the diagnosis to my sister, my mom and my dad. "Mrs. Kenan has a condition called ALS, also known as Lou Gehrig's disease. Best-case scenario, she has 18 months to live. Most likely, within a year, she will have no mobility and will require a ventilator to breathe."

Talk about a heart-stopping moment; my family didn't even know enough to ask intelligent questions about this disease we'd never heard of before. We took our cues from the physician who tried his best to provide details as his own heart was clearly breaking for our family.

"This disease attacks the nervous system and it gets progressively worse over time," he managed to explain. "Eventually, its victims become unable to move, speak, eat or even breathe on their own. There is no cure. She is so beautiful, and this should not be happening to her. But whatever dreams she had, anything on her bucket list, it needs to happen now."

We heard what the doctors said – there was nothing we could do about ALS but watch the matriarch of our family die. It shook us for a moment. But it didn't shake our faith.

"No. We are going to anoint her with oil, pray through this, and she will be healed!" we declared in Jesus' name. "You will be the next miracle, and this will be a testimony to once again demonstrate God's power."

We did all the things that the Bible says to do: "Touch and agree." "Declare a thing." "Speak it into existence." "Speak of things that be not as though they are." We lived on that Word. We stood on it. We trusted in the scriptures that say, "With God, all things are possible." We not only had to be faith-filled for ourselves, but also for my mom. So, our house became even more inundated with the Word of God. My dad led the church in a congregational fast, we put on our healing capes, and the gloves were on. We were ready to fight. We knew it was going to be a hard battle, but we believed in God who could do anything.

After my mom received an official diagnosis in November 2008, her condition rapidly declined in just one month. By Christmas she was almost totally immobile. Once she digested the idea that she was dying, it was hard for her to muster the fight to live.

We tried to keep the energy high and upbeat to lift her spirits and stave off depression. Every day my sister styled her hair and applied her makeup. We even did fun things like conducting mock interviews about her future miraculous healing. "Mrs. Kenan, how did you come through this tremendously trying ordeal?" we'd ask while shoving pretend microphones in her face. "Come on now; we have to get your testimony together!" She'd laugh and push our hands away. At the time, that laughter seemed as powerful as any cure or medicine.

Although her spirits and mind were strong, her body failed more and more each day. By this time, Sharnette had become my mother's full-time caregiver. She and my father spared no expense or self-sacrifice to make my mother as comfortable as possible. From buying an eye-tracking computer interface that would allow her to communicate "yes," "no" and other words with the blink of an eye, to sitting with her for hours while she consumed one bowl of soup through a straw. My sister and my dad were absolutely amazing; they never left her side and they never lost faith. "God, I believe you. Even in the midst of what I see, I still believe You," my father constantly prayed.

My obligations to the church and school system in Chattanooga didn't afford me the opportunity to stay in Texas full time. However, my younger sister Shanda and I took turns traveling to Midland on many weekends to pitch in with my mother's care. My brother Cersle, my brother-in-love Michael and my God sister Dameshia also provided tremendous support by calling, visiting and offering assistance any way they could.

On Mother's Day 2009, my siblings, my children and I gathered in Midland at my parents' home to celebrate the holiday. We assembled around the dinner table, offered grace for our meal and thanked God for our blessings just as we had always done year after year. Except this time, things were different. In that moment, my mother began crying.

"What's wrong, mom?" I asked.

By then, she had lost much of her ability to speak and it was difficult to decipher her words. But eventually she managed to mumble, "I won't be here." She knew she was losing her battle with ALS and understood that this could very well be her last Mother's Day.

"Oh Mama, don't say that! You *will* be here for another Mother's Day."

She dropped her head and sobbed uncontrollably. I reached down to console her with a hug and that's when the spirit of God revealed that she indeed would see her last days in less than a year. I didn't utter a word to my siblings about my revelation because we were still fighting. Instead, I was more resolved to being present every moment I could.

Initially, my sister Shanda and I began visiting Texas on alternating weekends to give Sharnette a break. As my mom's condition worsened, I flew there every week. I spent my savings, accepted donations and love offerings, and scraped together every penny I could find to purchase my $625 plane tickets. The airline employees knew me by name and did all they could to support me, even one night holding the plane when I arrived late to the Atlanta airport for a Friday evening departure. My employer was amazingly supportive allowing me to work from home as the Director of Student Services. They permitted me to conduct school transfer approvals by mail, submit reports electronically and perform many of my duties remotely. My church village stepped in, once again, and supported me during this time and helped me with my kids while I was frequently out of town.

In one of the most challenging moments of my life, it felt like everyone in my village was generous and accommodating to my situation. For that, I will forever be grateful. It taught me that God won't always change our circumstances, but he'll accommodate it. He helps us through a process of reconciliation with the harsh reality of what we're experiencing.

The reality I was facing was losing my best friend. She was slowly deteriorating in front of my face, and there was nothing I could do about it. The woman who I talked to every day and who showed me how to be a dedicated and loving helpmate to my spouse; the amazing woman whose spontaneous trips to the spa I sponsored and who I baked homemade sweet potato pies with on every holiday; and more important than anything, this was the woman who loved me from birth and taught me how to be a servant of God. Although her life journey was ending, I was being granted time to say goodbye.

One of the weekends that I was in Midland to give my older sister a break from being a caregiver, my mother and I shared a moment I will remember forever. I was careful to maintain her daily schedule which was important to keep her body – and mind – on a routine. We had a full day, starting with breakfast at 9 a.m., measured liquid intakes throughout the day, and periodic sessions to stretch her arms and legs to keep her limbs moving. At night, it was time to bathe her. Because her muscles were hardening like rocks all over her body, administering her baths required me to climb into the tub to lift her in and out – even though she outweighed me by 50 lbs., and the extra weight from the water didn't help. This particular night, when I went to lift her out of the water, I slipped, hit my head, and she and I both crashed down into the tub.

"Oh Sherry, I'm so sorry," my mother said as she cried.

"No, Mom. Don't be sorry. That's what we're here for! It's going to be okay. We're just going to lay here in this water and sing. 'Wade in the water!'" My head throbbed and I was sure I had a concussion, but that night I sang, laughed and cried with my mom. It was the perfect symbolism of my mental state.

I experienced wild swings in my emotions while watching my mother fight for her life. At times I was angry with God. I questioned Him. "God, are you *really* going to let this happen?!

You're going to let her sharp mind be trapped in a failing body and she's a prisoner in her own body? The one thing she loves to do is praise You; why are You letting that be taken away?"

Most of my conversations with God were intense and out loud. Sometimes I would be in the hospital hallway. Other times we'd "come to blows" in the living room of my mom and dad's home where I'd pace the floor, punch pillows and pour out my entire heart.

"God, this is not fair!" I said with raw emotion. "You promised that above all You wished we would be in health and our souls would prosper. You declared that you are our Healer. You promised us three scores and 10 years; that's 70 years. My mom is only 67. There are murderers and molesters thriving every day; why would You allow this to happen to someone who loves You?!"

The thing I love about God is He is big enough to handle these types of conversations. He is big enough to handle all of our disappointments and all of our tantrums. While some might say, "Be careful honey, God is going to strike you down." I believe He gives us grace to voice our anger. He let me vent on so many occasions and when I was done, I could hear him gently say, "Okay, now that you got that out, are you better now? At the end of the day, remember that I am God. I love you, and I love her. And I love all of My creation."

In a moment of loss, anguish and pain, it is imperative to strike a – seemingly impossible – balance between seeking our own desires and accepting God's sovereign will. I prayed every day for my mother's healing. Even though God had revealed her ultimate fate to me on Mother's Day, I knew that prayers from believers had the power to even change God's mind. I remembered the example of Hezekiah in the Old Testament whose life was extended by 15 years simply because he asked God for it. Yes, I wanted to have my mother longer. But I also wanted another demonstration of God's power.

"God, show the people! Show that faithfulness really does make a difference; that we can stand strong in faith and praying and believing, and we can see the hand of God turn in our favor! Nothing is too hard for You. I know You are no respecter of persons. You did it for Hezekiah, please do it now."

But no matter the outcome, I was resolved that God is God, and I would yield to His will.

"Whatever You allow, Lord, I'm good with it. I'm not going to turn my back on You. I will never walk away."

On September 2, 2009, Bertha Lee Bright Kenan, known affectionately by those who love her as Me-Maw, lost her battle with amyotrophic lateral sclerosis and passed away while my father and sister Sharnette slept at her bedside. She was 67 years old and had been married to my father William Cersle Kenan for 40 years. A part of me died that day, and I will never be the same. I never got over it, but I got *through* it with my siblings, my brother-in-love, my God sister, my children, my family and my church village.

More than 1,200 people attended the celebration of her life and countless individuals testified about how my mother saved their lives and blessed their families. She made a lasting impact and her kingdom work was done.

My siblings and I sang the Clark Sisters' song, "Is My Living In Vain" at my mother's celebration of life. In her case, of course the answer to that question is, "No!" She left the world better than it was when she entered it. What more can we ask for? Her service was beautiful, and she looked fabulous! The choir sang, "soon and very soon, we are going to see the king," as the procession exited the sanctuary. Even in our immense sadness, we knew she fought a good fight and finished her course.

When Loss Happens
Live Anyway
Accept What God Allows

- **Don't Run From The Pain.** How does one overcome the colossal weight of loss that seems unbearable? First, give yourself permission to feel the pain. Accept the truth and resist the urge to live in denial of what is happening. Denial can be detrimental. Instead, verbalize how you feel and have faith that God will grant you the leniency to express your pain to Him.

- **Keep Moving.** Don't grieve to the point of stagnation and perpetually long for what once was. Acknowledge that life now has a new norm. Instead of grieving the old norm, chart out what you will do in its place. When my mother passed away, I could no longer call her every day on my lunch break. Instead, I started meeting close friends for lunch dates. These friends were not replacements, rather they were ways to fill a void.

- **Redirect Your Energy.** Channel your grief and turn it into something positive. For me, my greatest testament was to honor my mother by *living*. I knew there was still more in me to accomplish, and I knew that walking in my calling would be my best tribute to her. It saddens me that she is not here to see me be a pastor, but her picture sits in my office today. She wasn't in the university arena to witness me earn my doctorate, but the day I walked across the stage, I wore the shoes that she gave me. Let the inspiration and motivation from those you have lost carry you into your future. Live a life that would make them proud even if they are absent from the body and unable to be physically present.

- **Trust God.** Don't turn your back on God just because you don't understand your circumstance. As humans, we ask questions that are reasonable to mankind such as, "why do bad things happen to good people?" To that I say, accept that God knows more than we do, and we'll understand better by and by. We don't have an answer for everything. Sometimes all I can say is, "I know He loves me and is a good God. But this right here? I can't explain it." Know that He is a sovereign God. There are things that He knows that we don't know. There are things He sees that we don't see. He is who He says He is. He is a healer, but every healing may not take place on this side; some healing will take place on the other side.

- **Accept What God Allows.** The Bible teaches us that God does not make people sick, but He will *allow* sickness. When sin entered the earth, it brought sickness, disease and death along with it, and mankind has to navigate these unpleasant experiences until we depart this life. God won't stop everything, even though He has the power to. But He has promised to never forsake us as we endure. In your quest for answers, seek the One who is the answer. Lean not to your own understanding and He will direct your path.

- **Focus On Eternity.** Find peace in the thought that the Bible tells us no one is here to stay forever. A man is born of a woman and that of a few days. We are pilgrims passing through. We have to make sure we do our work because no one gets out of here alive! Death and loss help us to come to grips with why we are really here; we live this life so we can live again. Remember all the good you've been blessed with and don't place all significance on one incident. My mother lived 66 years to the fullest. Her last year on this earth did not negate her entire life's work.

SCRIPTURE AND PRAYER

Naked I came from my mother's womb, and naked shall I return. The Lord gave, and the Lord has taken away; blessed be the name of the Lord.

Job 1:21

Trust in the Lord with all your heart, and do not lean on your own understanding. In all your ways acknowledge him, and he will make straight your paths.

Proverbs 3:5-6

Dear God,

Thank You for my mother who lived a life that was easy to celebrate and who gifted me with an inheritance of an unshakeable faith. Thank You for her wonderful example of what living a purposeful life looked like. I'm grateful for the opportunity to have enjoyed every moment I had with her. Help me to walk in Your will as I honor her memory.

Forgive me for my anger and questioning Your will. May Your grace and mercy cover me in my foolish moments. Forgive me for my tantrums and for my fleshly desire to try to manipulate Your will.

Help me do my work every day. Help me to live out my mother's legacy instead of dwelling in her demise. When I have fought this good fight of faith, if it doesn't turn out how I want, help me to accept what I can not change. Please allow me to fully submit to Your will and help me to accept what You allow. Amen.

7

When Failure Happens
Be Honest With Yourself

After we all learned to cope with losing my mom, little did I know that I would soon face the prospect of another crushing defeat: the loss of my marriage. I remember every excruciating moment as if it all just happened yesterday.

It was late summer of 2013, and we were preparing for a new school year that was scheduled to start in a few weeks. I was Director of Student Services for Hamilton County and my department was charged with overseeing the student registration process for the district. I was at the Central Office and I had a boardroom full of students, parents and social workers who were trying to execute transfers and resolve registration documentation issues. Hundreds of students were served every day for a month as we reviewed and processed about 10,000 requests for student transfers every year. It was the busiest time of the year for me, so when my baby sister Shanda called my cell phone that day, I was not at all prepared for the conversation we were about to have.

"Are you alright?" she asked with grave concern in her voice.

"Girl, yes, I'm alright," I answered hurriedly. "It's just a madhouse over here. We're trying to get everyone registered for school."

"Well, why would you be doing that right now?" she asked with an incredulous tone.

"Umm…because that's my job, Shanda. Why are you asking weird questions?"

"So you haven't heard? Sheryl, I am going to send you a link to an article that you need to see right now," she said.

"I really don't have time to look at a…"

"Sheryl. Stop!" she interrupted me. "I need you to look at this right now."

Impatiently and reluctantly, I grabbed my phone and clicked the link my sister sent. It led me to an article on a salacious website, and the headline was horrifying.

Former Chattanooga Pastor Exposed, Preacher Lives Double Life

Attached to the blog article were graphic photos of my husband that he had taken in our home and posted on online chatrooms and websites. There were also screenshots of conversations with him and other men who were advertising themselves and seeking sexual encounters.

Before I had time to fully digest what I was reading, I was called away to assist another student with school registration. I had to pull it together – just as I had done my whole life – while my entire world had just imploded.

As I made my way back to the boardroom where my work was waiting for me, anger rose from my feet to my head. *How could this be possible?! There must be some sort of mistake,* I thought.

The article must have been posted that morning, and I had been oblivious to the conversations that were swirling around about me. I imagine everyone was trying to figure out how to approach me about it. As the day went on, calls to my cell phone flooded in one right after another from my sisters, co-laborers from the ministry and many others. They were all assuring me that everything would be okay, but that was a tough sell for me in the moment.

Our marriage hadn't been right for a long time. But I was genuinely shocked that it had gone this far. I knew the intimacy was gone, he disappeared for days at a time, and there were unsubstantiated rumors that had haunted me for years. Gossip about my relationship was not uncommon. For example, an acquaintance once told me, "I saw your husband at a gay bar in Atlanta," when he was supposed to be traveling for evangelism engagements at churches. In another instance, a stranger called my home and said, "I just think you should know the truth. I'm in a relationship with your husband." But after every strange occurrence, I always turned to my spouse for answers.

"These people are just jealous of us, Sheryl," my husband would always reassure me. "They want what we have: success, local prominence and a beautiful family. Don't listen to these people who are only trying to tear us down. We have to stick together."

Well, we had not been *together* in a long time. But with all the years of loneliness and insecurity, I still never had *proof* of marital misconduct – the one thing that would have constituted a legitimate termination of my marriage in the opinion of many of my church leaders, parishioners and family members. Not until this day.

This public disclosure of my husband's secret behavior confirmed what before had only been speculation. It was in black and white, and I couldn't reason it away, dismiss it or chalk it up to murmuring from the peanut gallery.

At some point, my anger turned to myself. Sometimes failure happens at no fault of our own, when we've done nothing wrong. Sometimes we are forced to be honest and confess how we contributed to our own failure. Many times, it's a combination of both.

For years, I buried the hints and clues about my husband's demons. I covered them with busyness so I wouldn't have to face the reality that I was miserable. It was my coping mechanism. I ran myself into the ground so I wouldn't have time to care about being lonely. I expended all my energy on caring for our children, leading the church, advancing my career and being a source of strength for my mother, father and siblings. After years of investing mental and emotional currency on trying to save my marriage and save my husband from himself, I was spent. Consequently, I had become desensitized and callous to the terrible marriage in which I was merely existing. Had I been in denial to the truth all along? Was I to blame for accepting his behavior for over a decade? Regardless, this day was an appalling reckoning with the truth.

When I finally got my husband on the phone, I erupted.

"I can not believe you!" I screamed to the top of my lungs while standing in the parking lot of my office building.

"But Sheryl, I told you," he defended himself. "I told you something was coming!"

"No sir. You did not say *this* was coming!"

A week before the article was published, my husband had initiated a sit-down, face-to-face conversation at home. He explained that someone was trying to blackmail him with a bunch of lies and it was going to come out publicly. Without going into any details – like so many of our conversations – he just implored that we stick together even if what happened was bad. I had no indication that it would be this devastating. I figured it would be similar shenanigans that he'd pulled in the past, and we'd find a way to work through it once again. I now understand that conversation was his attempt to warn me, but the gulf between us had grown so wide I couldn't hear him.

While standing in the parking lot of my job, his words from our previous conversation a week prior had new meaning and the context was now painfully clear.

"I tried to tell you," he repeated. "Just like I tried to tell you back then, I tried to tell you now!"

"What *then*?! What are you talking about?!" I was irate and tears streamed down my face.

"I told you from the beginning," he said. "Before we got married, I told you I couldn't do this. And I tried to tell you again the other day. I can't do this!"

It took me a long time – 18 years – to connect the dots. Two weeks before our wedding, my fiancé came to me and said, "I'm not sure I can do this."

"What are you saying?" I was confused.

In retrospect, I now know he was trying to tell me, *I'm not the guy you think I am. I'm battling with things I don't know how to deal with.* But the only thing he could manage to articulate was "I just can't do it."

Instead of listening to and interpreting his words back then in 1995, I immediately became defensive. "So, you don't love me? We've promoted this wedding, we've paid for all these things...and now you're going to tell me you don't love me?!"

"No, Sheryl, I love you," he said while crying. "That's why I can't do this."

"Is there someone else that you want to be with? Do you have cold feet? I don't understand! Why have you been lying to me?" I besieged him with questions.

After an intense back and forth, he conceded. "Never mind. I shouldn't have said anything at all. I love you. We're good."

"So, it's just cold feet then?"

"Yeah, cold feet," he replied. "That's all it is. We're okay."

I got married at age 25. I was still somewhat sheltered from many of the ways of the world and, having had very few adult relationships, I didn't fully grasp all the nuances of dating. My thinking two weeks before my wedding was, *you're saying you love me but you're pulling this stunt?! Those two things don't go together.*

But in all actuality, they somewhat did. In that moment, he was trying to love me the best way he knew how. He would rather ruin my year by breaking things off with me two weeks before my wedding than destroy my entire life by entering into a marriage under false pretenses.

However, he never gave me all the pieces to the puzzle. He never said, *I can't do this because I'm broken; I can't do this because I'm the product of abuse; I can't do this because I don't know what a good marriage is supposed to look like.*

After I had time to sit in my quiet space and reflect, I finally realized all the things he was actually trying to tell me. He was trying to spare me from everything that he didn't have a handle on. He knew he couldn't live up to the model of marriage I had seen from my parents, and he didn't know how or take the time to learn how to be a good husband. Instead of bringing me into his mess, he just wanted to bail. But that didn't work, because I didn't let him off the hook.

So, his next effort was to sabotage our marriage. He would rather I hate him because he was a bad husband who walked out on me than hate him for discovering who he really was on the inside. He tried several times to push me out of the door and leave him, but my loyalty wouldn't let me just walk away.

"I'm not going anywhere," was my standard response.

"What is wrong with you? A normal person would be gone! You should hate me," he would say. And it was true. I put up with way more than I should have. Over the course of 18 years, he had largely abdicated his duties as a husband. Not once did he visit my mother when she was dying, he disappeared for days and weeks at a time, and would only show up to preach at church on Sunday. From covering for him after countless disappearing acts to denying the rumors that he was living with other people when he wasn't home with me and the kids, I never left him. There are people who think I should've hated him, but I just saw him as a wounded person.

"I don't know how to give up on people," I told him. "I just don't." Just like I didn't walk out on the kids who were trying to set fires at my first teaching job at the middle school in Chattanooga. Neither did I immediately leave the church whose members voted us out of leadership. In similar fashion, I stayed with my husband. I put on my missionary hat, and decided to be there for him like no one had been before. I decided to love him the way he needed to be loved, because I thought love could solve all our problems. A good woman can cure everything, right?

I was so wrong. There were wounds in my husband's psyche from his past that were not healed. Other people had witnessed them all along the way, but had not encouraged him to seek help. Many times in society, we'd rather cover up people's demons and shortcomings instead of usher them to healing. I was not the first person to see my husband's monsters, but others taught him it was shameful to expose your weaknesses, and urged him to keep his struggles a secret. The only problem with that approach is that people who refuse to embrace and acknowledge their brokenness can never be healed. So, his issues did nothing but fester, metastasize and bubble to the surface.

As the layers started being pulled back, I began to see who he really was. And part of my job then became doing what I was upset with everyone else about – covering for him. I wanted to help him maintain his image of the charismatic evangelist even though at home I knew he was perpetuating the generational behavior of emotional abuse. I was committed to supporting him. I suggested that he seek professional help all while being careful not to utter a word to anyone outside of our household – not even to my family – for fear that they would have a diminished opinion of him. I was trying to be a team player and get through it together. But in reality, the more I tried to get everyone to buy into the facade, the more things fell apart. Eventually, I submitted to the truth that you can't help someone who doesn't want to be helped and has no desire to change.

The day my husband's exploits hit the internet was one of the lowest points in my life. It almost broke me. I was forced to honestly evaluate where I was and determine how I was going to move forward. It was one of my toughest challenges. But had that day not happened, something equally or more drastic would have had to occur for me to wake up and acknowledge the truth about my situation.

Adding even more insult to injury, we were a high-profile couple and all our drama played out on a public stage. I've always known that the higher you ascend in society, the harder you fall. But I never could have imagined that falling from grace in public view would be so hurtful, humbling and, frankly, humiliating. Our failure was laid bare for all the world to see. Everyone who had witnessed our ascension to popularity over the last decade now had a front-row seat to our spectacular demise. So, it was no surprise when a media team from a local news station showed up at my church seeking to interview me about the scandal. One of my top priorities was to protect my children from harm during this time, and this moment put that plan to the test. A member of our church who was also a police officer routinely helped us with security. He immediately spotted the reporter's arrival on our grounds. He met her at the front door and denied her entry as my children and I were rushed out of the back. Having no success in her bid to speak to me at church, the reporter vowed to catch me at my job. Within a matter of days, she made good on her threat, but was turned away by my supervisor.

"Sir, we are pursuing a story about one of your employees and we would like to speak with her," the reporter said.

"The only stories we have here are school-related," my supervisor sternly responded. "If you are on campus for any matter other than school business, you are not welcome."

The thought of how this must have looked from an outsider's point of view was embarrassing. My image of "Perfect Sherry" was under attack, and I anticipated all the people who would relish the opportunity to say, "I told you so." Even some of my closest family members never wanted us to get married in the first place.

This was one of many experiences where I am appreciative of my world unraveling. I believe things had to fall apart to the point where I could no longer cover for my husband or pretend my marriage was good, or else I'd still be in it. I didn't take this as a sign of God being mad at me and I didn't have the attitude of *why did He let this happen to me?* I honestly had more of a spirit of *Thank you, God. It's out there; it's all in the open.* There was no more hiding the truth that my marriage had been in shambles for years. I could exhale.

Was I angry? Of course. I was ticked off! But at the same time,

I was relieved. It might seem crazy but, even though this situation was painful, I was finally free from the pressures that had weighed on me throughout my marriage. There was nothing left to hide. Nothing to protect. Nothing to defend.

I couldn't clean it up. I couldn't explain it away. It was out there.

When Failure Happens
Live Anyway
Be Honest With Yourself

- **Deal With The Truth.** Sometimes, the truth hurts, and the brain builds a defense mechanism to help you disassociate from reality so that you can function. Sometimes my friends tell me about things that happened in my darkest moments and I will honestly not remember them. I would have blocked it out just to make it through. But there comes a time when you must deal with your issues. Don't live in denial. If you don't properly deal with the truth, then you can convince yourself to believe a lie. Don't ignore red flags or warning signs that you are given, and understand that you can never heal from wounds that you don't acknowledge and properly address.

- **Work On Yourself.** Don't blame yourself when failure happens, but evaluate your role in it. Identify, discuss and work on your behaviors and character flaws that contributed to your situation. For me, my total loyalty and devotion to people has always been a blessing. But when it becomes self-sacrificing, it can also be a curse.

My loyalty was damaging, because I was choosing to go down with a sinking ship instead of escaping on a life raft in the interest of self-preservation. Take an honest look at how you can improve your circumstances by adjusting your attitude and your actions.

- **Don't Get Stuck.** It's easy to get caught up in what went wrong, but don't wallow in the mire of defeat. Yes, it is important to comprehensively assess the damage after we have been unsuccessful. But it's even more important to move forward in a healthy manner. Perform an autopsy of the failed relationship, venture or project, and be proactive to determine measures that will prevent you from making the same mistakes in the future.

- **Know That You Are Not A Failure.** If you've never failed, then you've probably never taken risks, stepped outside of your comfort zone, or attempted something that has the potential for great reward. One consequence of striving for greatness is that you will one day miss the mark. Dealing with that setback in public makes it doubly disappointing. But know that your failures do not define you. Pick yourself up after each stumble, regroup and reset your aim for your next goal.

SCRIPTURE AND PRAYER

Fear not, for I am with you; be not dismayed, for I am your God; I will strengthen you, I will help you, I will uphold you with my righteous right hand.

Isaiah 41:10

But he said to me, 'My grace is sufficient for you, for my power is made perfect in weakness.' Therefore, I will boast all the more gladly of my weaknesses, so that the power of Christ may rest upon me. For the sake of Christ, then, I am content with weaknesses, insults, hardships, persecutions, and calamities. For when I am weak, then I am strong.

2 Corinthians 12:9-10

Father,

Thank You for being the lifter of my head. You did not promise me success all the time, but You did promise that You would never forsake me. I realize that a season of failure isn't always about becoming a stronger person as much as it is about trusting a stronger God.

Forgive me when I am in denial of the truth and I delay dealing with my shortcomings. Please bless me with good judgement so that I can honestly evaluate my flaws and learn from my missteps. Help me to turn my failures into opportunities to grow wiser. Thank You for giving me the strength to get back up and try again, even when it hurts, and grant me the courage to keep moving forward every day. Amen.

8

When Depression Happens
Ask For Help

If there was ever a time when I experienced emotional imbalance, it was during this period of my life. Although I was relieved from the pressure of pretending to be happy, I was also grieving my marriage. Even though I subconsciously wanted a way out of my misery, my very public failure felt like the cruelest demise imaginable. My entire spirit had grown cold and numb, but every passing thought of the embarrassment I'd just endured felt like a punch to the gut.

Ultimately, I collapsed under the weight of my defeat and succumbed to my darkest notions. I no longer had the desire to force myself to carry on. For years, I had buried my pain and put one foot in front of the other to survive my troubled marriage day by day. But I no longer had the desire to summon any strength to fight. I conceded to the crushing conquest of failure and it reigned over me. Albeit temporary, it was a total and absolute surrender.

The public disclosure of my marriage troubles was the tipping point. Things before had injured me, but nothing had broken me. I didn't know it was possible to feel worse than I did when my mom died, but this came close. At least when that happened, I was still able to muster the energy to keep going by leaning into my "strong Sherry" role. But now, I was completely exposed. My humanness and my weakness were visible, and I could no longer conceal any of it.

During this time when everything came crashing down, there

was a span of days when I didn't leave my home. For me, those few days were more like a month because such behavior was so far outside of my character. I had a real breakdown. I was finally facing the summit of years of never properly dealing with all my grief and emotional abuse.

I refused to eat, get out of bed, bathe or be around anyone. Chattanooga is not a big city. At any given time, you can go to a local store or restaurant and see someone you know. I was well-known in the city and didn't want to go anywhere at all. My family and friends repeatedly tried to reach me by phone, but I declined the calls. I didn't want to talk to anyone, because I didn't have an explanation for anything that was happening.

There were very few people who I allowed in my home at that time; Sparka was one of them. Although we met in a church setting when she was a college student attending Living Word Ministries, Sparka became deeply rooted in my personal life. She was like an aunt to my children and frequently helped with them when I traveled or had an overbooked schedule. During the difficult time of my mother's illness, she was right by my side, even occasionally accompanying me on the 16-hour drive from Chattanooga to Midland on the weekends that I did not catch a flight.

Sparka is like family to me, and during this period of time when I was isolated at home, it was difficult for me to even respond to her. When she came over each morning to help get the kids off to school, she spoke to me, but the words fell on deaf ears as if she weren't saying anything at all. When she turned on the lights in the bedroom where I was hibernating, I covered my head with the bedding and said, "leave me alone." She pleaded with me to eat. "If nothing else, can you please at least drink something?" she implored. I simply wouldn't respond.

She witnessed all of my humiliation and depression firsthand. She knew my behavior was not normal, and thank God, she took action.

One morning after dropping my children off at school, she took a vacation day from her job and returned to my home. After days of no response from me and my refusal to get out of bed, she did the only thing she knew to do to bring me back to life; she pulled the cover and bed linens off of my body and splashed me with a cup full of water.

"You are going to come out of this!" she declared. "You have two children who are depending on you, and you will not be stuck in this!"

Although I was shocked she had done this, I still didn't react. I felt the water but continued to just stare at the ceiling as she began praying over me.

"God, please bring Pastor Sheryl back to us. Keep her mind, Lord."

It wasn't until she told me about her conversation with my daughter that I snapped out of it.

"Sheridan came to me crying today," Sparka told me. "She is worried about you and doesn't know what is going on. She said, 'my mom just won't get up. She won't even take a bath!'"

At that moment, a switch in me flipped. My children were my world, and I was failing them. My daughter was scared, and I wasn't shielding her from my pain, as I had done all her life. Even though I was trying to hold my own mind together with a rubber band, I still had an obligation to protect my children.

All they had ever seen from me was a positive attitude that exuded "everything is great," and "we're going to be fine." That was my normal modus operandi. My son and daughter believed that *"Mama will take care of everything." "Mama is a superhero." "Mama is literally Super Woman."* They had never seen me in this state.

While they didn't know the details of what had transpired, my daughter knew that her father had done something very serious to upset me. Unfortunately, I could no longer hide my trauma from my children.

Hearing that my daughter was distraught by my current state provided a jolt to my system that I desperately needed. I knew I had to get myself together, and do it fast, whether I felt like it or not. I needed to prove to the world – and most importantly, to myself – that I was still strong. In that moment, Sparka helped me out of bed. I took a bath, drank some juice and decided I had to live anyway.

This was not my first brush with depression. I was depressed after I had a stroke at age 28 and after being voted out of church leadership. I quit sleeping, and paced the floor all night, learning how to operate on adrenaline. Many times throughout my marriage, I sat in my car on a bridge at the Chickamauga Dam overlooking the Tennessee River. I was just plain tired, and I contemplated how I could end all my sorrows with one plunge into the dark, cold river. Although I never attempted to take my own life, I had a newfound understanding and compassion for those who have. *I get it*, I reasoned within myself.

Sometimes, I fantasized about driving down Interstate 75 South and never coming home. Just like the many times my husband disappeared for weeks fulfilling his desire to "get away" and "be free." But I didn't have that luxury. *Who's gonna feed the kids?! I can't leave them no matter how bad things are for me.*

Other times, after I tucked the children into bed for the

night, I would leave them and their father at home while I took some time to be alone. I'd drive to the local Walmart parking lot and sit in my car all night thinking, *I can't live like this.* It had all become too much. I couldn't see the light at the end of the tunnel. All the work I had done to protect my "perfect" image had been in vain; it did nothing but blow up in my face. I was constantly berated by the person I was trying to help, all while trying to uphold the appearance that "everything is good." I was a married single mom who worked tirelessly at my day job and had loads of responsibilities at church, but there were times I felt invisible in my own home. I had nowhere to lay my head, no solace. My home was not a place of peace. So, I found peace in random places like sitting in the car in retail store parking lots in the middle of the night. In my time alone, I would think, pray, cry and have an all-out, raging pity party.

I was upset with God. *Lord, I don't understand. I dedicated my life to You for this? I preach every day to people who are being delivered and being blessed, but I go home so broken. Lord, I don't know what to do with this. Other people are being ushered to their wholeness yet I'm still in pieces!*

I was angry at myself.

I resented the fact that I couldn't just be normal. I was mad about being a leader and having responsibilities. I hated it. I just wanted to be an everyday person with no one counting on me. *I don't want to hear your problems. I have my own. I don't want to have to pray you through it. I'm trying to figure out how to pray for myself.*

I started dreading conversations about people who were in healthy relationships. *I don't want to hear stories about how someone loves and cares about you, or about how they miss you when you're not there. Go tell somebody who cares. I don't care!*

I solved problems for people at church and at my job all the time. People came to me for help, and all I wanted to do was cry on their shoulders. I wanted to say, *I'm done with all this. I don't want to be a pastor who puts on an amazing public performance in the pulpit, but my whole life shuts down by the time I get to the car. I don't want to be a principal. I don't want to be a director. I don't want to be any of this.*

Although I didn't know how to fix my situation, I did the one thing I knew how to do; I prayed. I knew to go to God. I knew if I was going to climb out of this deep ravine, it was going to be through Him. Looking back, I know I should have sought professional counseling. I'm not sure my fight would have been as hard had I received help because it would have given me the tools that I needed to properly manage my depression. But through it all, I was driven to my knees before God's throne, I dove into scripture and I reminded myself of what I had been taught all my life: *Put the Word in motion and exercise your faith through action.*

After each night of self-pity and prayer in the Walmart parking lot, I always gave myself a pep talk just as the sun peeked over the horizon.

This is your life, Sheryl. This is what you've got. You are going to keep moving. There are two little people depending on you; your two greatest gifts on this earth.

I'd get home just in time to get them up, get them ready for school and tell them with a smile on my face, "Let's go. It's going to be a great day."

I was in a fog for a very long time during this latest bout with depression. I felt like I couldn't pray my way out of the funk I was in. I strangely tried to become my own therapist. I re-read my old sermons, referenced guidance I had counseled other people with in the past, and tried to bring myself back to life with my own advice. But self-therapy wasn't enough.

I finally asked my friend Terri for help while sitting in the booth of a local restaurant. She and I had been buddies for years. We met in an educational setting, as she is a certified counselor in the school system. People would say we look alike, and our last names started with the same letter; so, naturally, we claimed each other as sisters. We were always swapping silly stories about maxing out our credit cards on shopping trips, discussing the challenges and joys of motherhood or simply sharing a quick laugh amid our crazy busy schedules. She is a married woman of faith who is close to my age. We had many things in common and it was easy for us to connect on an authentic level.

When my marriage crumbled, I knew I could trust and depend on her. I called her and said, "I need help. Things are just not good. I've tried to cope with my depression on my own, trying to protect my image, but I feel like I am about to blow up."

I remember the day we met at Panera like we had done many times before, but this particular day, everything had changed. "Oh, my friend! How are you? How is everything going?" she greeted me.

I sank into the corner booth and I told my friend the truth. I cried as I told her every ugly detail. I divulged all the nitty-gritties about my marriage, more than what could be found on social media or news websites. It was the first time I ever became completely undone, and I wasn't ashamed. We sat in the booth until the restaurant closed, and then we stood in the parking lot for another two hours talking and crying. We were declaring and decreeing God's word over my situation, and she let me vent and bare my soul with no judgement. She simply listened and loved me through it.

That conversation with Terri at Panera started a cathartic release. It was the therapy I needed, and soon after that night, our meetings became more frequent. She'd come to my office at work, close the door and say, "How are we today, friend?" She'd send me prayers and affirmations in all capital letters in text messages. "YOU ARE ENOUGH. HOLD YOUR HEAD UP. GOD ALREADY KNEW AND HE EQUIPPED YOU TO HANDLE IT. YOU ARE BEAUTIFUL, STRONG AND AMAZING. LOVE YOU TO LIFE, FRIEND." We had periodic phone calls and check-ins, and she gave me strategies and routines that I needed to establish in my life. She taught me how to connect my feelings to a particular thing, place or time. She helped me reconcile the private me – who needed encouragement – and the public me – who was always the encourager. She taught me to be okay with living in duality, and she showed me how to do it in a healthy manner.

"When is our next session, Sheryl?" Terri would ask when not hearing from me for a few days.

"I know, we're overdue! What's my fee today?" I jokingly responded. Our time together was filled with laughter, crying and at times confusion. I was able to release all of my emotions and it was healing for me. We met often and for long periods of time. If we connected at 6 p.m., then I would come back home at midnight. I don't know if it qualified as treatment that can be documented in a clinical manner, but it helped, and it was just what I needed.

My friendship and conversations with Terri helped me get through a difficult time so that I could come back to myself. I needed a moment when I didn't have to help anybody, I didn't have to put on a face for anybody. She saw me in my rawness. Our sessions were a no-judgement zone, but a place to be nurtured back to health after being severely wounded. It got me to a place where I could say, "I'm good" again, and actually mean it.

When Depression Happens
Live Anyway
Ask For Help

- **Know When To Seek Help.** Everyone deals with a certain amount of sadness just from living. But how do you know when it's time to get help? I am not a mental health professional, and this is by no means intended to be therapeutic advice. However, it is important to recognize warning signs of a level of depression that could possibly jeopardize your health. My depression indicators were things like: being around people started to become painful so I always wanted to be alone; I started spending abnormal amounts of time at random places like store parking lots; I lost my appetite and didn't want to eat (a tactic the Enemy employs to try to take away our strength); and I simply stopped caring about how things turned out. Apathy can be a gateway to depression. If you find yourself constantly troubled with these and other types of unhealthy feelings, consider contacting an expert who is certified, licensed or trained to provide appropriate care.

- **Understand That Seeking Help Is Not Weakness.** Don't buy into the stigma that obtaining professional help is a sign of weakness. For years, I needed help, but I didn't seek it. Instead, I chose to maintain an image of what I thought portrayed strength. Unfortunately, there are numerous cultures and communities that do not embrace counseling. The church community sometimes promotes the idea that receiving counseling means you're not relying on God. Some social and ethnic communities perpetuate long-standing cultural perceptions that therapy means you have mental health issues, you're unstable, you're weak or you're losing your mind. Do not let anyone deter you from your self-care. Don't listen to naysayers who may say, "You don't need that. You're stronger than that." Sometimes we speak a strength into people that they are not equipped to stand in, and we push people to be something that they just are not. We see the visual of who we think they are, but we don't know the fight it takes for them to present that picture.

- **Select Your Confidants Wisely.** Do your research and be sure to put yourself in good hands. If you are depressed, then you are very vulnerable, and sadly, there are people who will take advantage of that. Select a trusted individual with an objective opinion who will be neutral, unbiased, attentive, confidential, and can hear what you're really saying. Even if you do not engage a certified or licensed therapist, you should still seek guidance from a confidant who has displayed previous examples of providing wise and helpful advice.

- **Jumpstart Your Healing With Counseling.** Sometimes we all need a little extra strength; just like a battery that isn't totally dead, but just needs a boost. Always remember that a dead battery can't boost another battery. Don't look for healing from other hurt people who are just as bad off as you are and would be content to swap sob stories and dig depression holes for each other. Guard your company even when you're in a dark place. Don't look to be pacified; look to be pushed. Find people, who are living purposefully and are bringing you life with their conversations, their actions and their spirits.

SCRIPTURE AND PRAYER

You keep him in perfect peace whose mind is stayed on you, because he trusts in you.

Isaiah 26:3

...casting all your anxieties on him, because he cares for you. Be sober-minded; be watchful. Your adversary the devil prowls around like a roaring lion, seeking someone to devour.

---

1 Peter 5:7-8

Father,

In my darkest moments, I call upon You and You hear my cry. You are all powerful and Your strength carries me when I am too weak to stand on my own. Thank You for soothing my troubled spirit with Your peace that surpasses all understanding. I give You my worry and in exchange You provide Your serenity and love.

Thank You for delivering me from the valley of depression and for the support of loved ones who picked me up after I had fallen. You preserved my mind and provided a way of escape so that I could find a way back to myself.

You are my everything, Lord. I love You, and I know You love me so much more than I could ever imagine. Help me to always turn to You and open my eyes to the avenues of help that You provide. Amen.

9

When "The End" Happens
Let Go And Move Forward

The book of Ecclesiastes reminds us that there is a season for beginnings and a season for endings. It's essentially the cycle of life and how everything in it works. In order to live and flourish in our next phase of life, we may have to dismiss some people we've entertained, uproot routines we've cultivated and tear down structures we've built.

Although endings are hard, life requires them. There is danger in fighting for something when it's time to move on. If we don't learn how to conduct necessary endings, then we stay stuck, miss out on opportunities, and fail to reach our goals and dreams. Sometimes fear makes us stay too long past our expiration date.

There are countless examples in my life when I could have avoided many hardships if I'd only had enough courage to let go much sooner.

A prime example is our church Living Word. Yes, we built it from scratch. Yes, it was our "baby" that afforded us once-in-a-lifetime opportunities to minister to the world and change lives. And yes, it was the place that gave rise to my calling as a pastor. But, by the time we officially shut it down, the church had already been dead for years.

Parishioners started leaving the congregation because it became apparent that my husband – the senior pastor – no longer wanted to be there. He no longer had a passion for the ministry, and people began to notice. He would be absent from the congregation for weeks at a time, and he began lashing out at people for no reason. One church member said to me, "People have choices to attend other churches. We don't have to come here and be abused!"

There was a constant power struggle in our church leadership. One moment my husband would make me the site pastor, then on a whim, would swoop in to take the church back under his stewardship.

Divisions in the church made it difficult to be at peace and carry out the Lord's mission. I tried – unsuccessfully – to referee and be the peacemaker between the flock and my husband.

People who had never attended church in their lives had become members at our church. People had left other congregations to follow us and were deeply committed to the ministry. That's who I was fighting for. I desperately wanted to hold everybody together.

Surely, Lord, you didn't let us build this ministry where so many families are blessed, and now it will dissolve into nothing?! I pondered.

At the height of Living Word Ministries, there were approximately 450 members and no less than 100 visitors every week. Near its end, we had 20 to 25 members. We fell apart literally and figuratively. The building itself was a historic structure built in 1899 and contractors warned us that it was becoming unstable. The ceiling was falling down, there was severe water damage, and if there were storms on a Sunday morning, I prayed that God would protect us from harm during the service that day.

Eventually it all just stopped working. After 14 years, we called the Tennessee Secretary of State in 2011, and dissolved Living Word Ministries. Then, I started Destiny Church of Chattanooga with the few remaining church members we had. My husband went to Florida to start a new ministry of his own. We sold the building that formerly housed Living Word for little to nothing, just for the remaining balance on the loan. Within months, the building collapsed, and the destruction was reported on local news outlets. No one was injured, but the legacy of the landmark church building had ended. The building was demolished a short time after and today it is an empty lot. I drive by on occasion and reminisce about the glory days.

It's not always clear when your expiration date is approaching or when you've reached the end of a season. But I have found that the harder I try to avoid necessary endings, the worse the fallout. Delaying the inevitable leaves us vulnerable to prolonged misery, fear, toxicity and emotional damage.

Removing ourselves from toxic people and situations is not always easy. I had another hard-knock lesson with this idea when it was clear my marriage had run its course and was beyond repair. I knew we were in a place that was near impossible to recover from, but I never wanted to be a divorcee. I always hoped we could have a "return from hell" story that I'd seen other couples experience. But that wasn't our fate, and it was hard for me to accept the finality of divorce.

The first time I met with my divorce lawyer, I was completely overwhelmed. My body was shaking as I walked through the door. Her hallway was probably no more than 10 feet long, but it felt like the longest walk ever. I sat down in her office, not knowing how the process worked, but I knew how I wanted it to end.

"I don't want anything from him," I told my lawyer. "I just want out."

"Are you sure you want to do this, Sheryl?" she asked. "I

understand how you are feeling, but let me walk you through all the scenarios that could happen and let's discuss your options.

"Because you have a more lucrative and stable career, you may have to pay spousal support to the tune of $1,500 every month."

Really? I thought to myself. *So, someone can betray me, provide no financial assistance to our children, yet I'm the one who has to pay spousal support? How is that fair?*

She continued.

"Sometimes in situations like this, people don't necessarily want their kids, but they will fight for them just to hurt you. So, begin thinking about how you will feel if a judge grants him custody of your children every other weekend."

That didn't sit well with me at all.

"Even with pictures like this?!" I screamed as I shoved my phone in her face, showing her the explicit blog posts from six months ago.

"His private life has nothing to do with whether he's a good father," she calmly replied. "Your husband has never hit the kids, and you've never filed formal complaints against him. Your children may be exposed to environments that you don't like, and there will be nothing you can do about it.

"Try to befriend him because the less hostile the dynamics between the two of you, the more likely decisions will be made out of reason and not emotion.

"Demonstrate your financial responsibility by paying off debt. The fewer possessions you have to separate, the better. Finances can get tied up in court for a long time. Try to put money aside for the kids and prove that you can take care of them. Gather all your receipts that show you've always been the support for them. Also, because your children are minors, you'll be required to attend parenting classes. You'll need to show that you've tried for at least six months to work through your marital issues via mediation."

This initial session with my lawyer was a sobering reality check. Ending my marriage was going to be a long road.

"So, I guess you can't just pay someone to go to court and everything is done, huh?" I asked.

"I know it's a lot, but I will be here with you every step of the way," she reassured me.

At the end of our meeting, we decided that a legal separation was a good first step. I signed the paperwork, gathered my belongings, and left my lawyer's office with my head spinning. *I don't think I can do this. Who wants to start their life all over when they're almost fifty years old? Maybe I can just stay legally separated forever,* I thought.

On the surface, an infinite separation was tempting. It kept my marriage technically intact and I wouldn't have to endure the headache of severing myself and all my possessions from the person I "became one" with over 20 years ago. It would satisfy my desire to never be divorced, and just maybe I could regain some of my dignity, self-respect and independence. On the other hand, I knew that wasn't a viable option because it left me legally tied to my husband in too many ways. If nothing else, the separation bought me time, and I used it to get my affairs in order.

We were stuck in the legal separation phase for years and it was incredibly frustrating on many fronts.

On one hand, it breathed hope into my husband that I would

stay with him.

"If you really wanted to be done, you'd divorce me already," he argued. "You don't want to do this. We can make it work. You know you really love me."

On the other hand, I endured judgement from my friends and church members who misinterpreted my decision to stay legally married. They delivered a steady barrage of unsolicited feedback and criticism.

"You must like being abused, because if you didn't, you would be out of this."

"Honey, are you scared to let go? Legally separated means y'all are still married."

"I hope you will finally see your worth and understand you deserve better than this."

"We can't trust you to pastor our congregation. It's obvious that you will go back to him at any given time."

There were others who didn't believe in divorce and tried to convince me to stay.

"Pastor, don't let the devil break what God has put together. Your husband made a mistake but that's what forgiveness is about."

Privately, I had battled for years with religious pressures to stay married. The denomination I grew up in teaches that divorce is wrong and against God's law. We were taught since childhood that God won't smile favorably on those who are divorced, and that without a male covering, a female preacher is outside of God's will.

My internal conflict about this issue was a huge factor that kept me in my marriage for a long time. My personal belief is that victims of unhealthy marriages where emotional or physical abuse is taking place should get out of there right away. But I knew the church frowned upon divorce. Instead, we were taught to pray and do everything possible to work it out because "the husband is sanctified by the sanctified wife." The interpretation and tradition I heard all my life was to hang in there and stick it out.

I was taught that the Bible only releases one from marriage under the circumstance of adultery. During my marriage, I prayed, *Father, give me documented, certified information so that the whole world will know that if I am divorced, then it is Biblically-based and I can walk free!*

Although I believed my husband's photos confirmed my suspicions of marital misconduct, he denied that the photos I'd seen were even real; he claimed they were digitally altered. *So, he's all over the internet and I still can't go?* I thought to myself.

Part of me wanted to make the divorce official to prove to everyone that I could let go. But somehow, staying married seemed to be a neutral zone where I didn't have to make any decisions that completely rocked the boat. Being legally separated seemed like a good – although temporary – solution. I was still married, but I got away from my husband. I could satisfy all sides and I hoped everyone would just leave me alone.

The separation gave me a safe space to rediscover myself. I was able to think clearly about how a divorce would affect me, my ministry and my children, and I weighed the pros against the cons. I wasn't fully swayed in either direction until one night a terrifying dream solidified my decision. I was submerged in a large body of water and was desperately fighting to resurface and stay afloat. The pressures of my life were weighing me down so much that I was drowning. Every time I frantically reached for objects that should have served as lifelines they actually functioned like anchors that made me sink further underwater. Suddenly, I was jarred out of my sleep and I jumped up from my bed. My dream was so vivid and lifelike that I had physiological responses; my body was drenched in sweat and my heart was racing. *All of this is happening because I can't decide if I should stay or go?!* I thought. *I'm so worried about what people think that I'm considering going back to an unhealthy environment? Oh no! I have to get out of here. This separation is done!*

In the end, I decided the only way for me to live and not die was to get out of the treacherous waters that I'd been trying to tread for so long. Being merely separated kept me tied to my past; if I was ever going to soar and boldly embark upon my future, then I had to sever the mental and emotional restraints that were holding me back. So, after three years of separation, I officially filed for divorce to end my marriage of 22 years.

To close out an already tumultuous season, I lost my highly lucrative job with Hamilton County Schools in 2017. My storied career full of accolades, acknowledgments and awards fizzled into the background as I exited the school system.

During the 23 years I was employed by Hamilton County, I served as a teacher, assistant principal, principal, coordinator, and a Director of Operations – where I concluded my experience. In that process, I was named a Turnaround Principal after increasing a school's proficiency by more than 400%; I was recognized by Tennessee Governor Don Sundquist for a progressive reading program that yielded tremendous academic results for urban children; I was recognized as the youngest principal in Hamilton County; I revamped the registration process for the entire school system; and I served as a general fire extinguisher putting out fires throughout the district. I was dedicated to supporting the educators, principals, parents and students, and I was devoted to the idea that we could change lives through education. I experienced the summit of my professional career here. But when my time was up, there was no longer a place for me. In a nutshell, the very people who I helped and mentored along the way made my last years at Hamilton County Schools a tortuous nightmare in what felt like a coordinated effort to push me out. The same ones who I'd championed, fought for and shown the ropes, were the very ones who got rid of me.

My last position was Director of Innovation Zone Schools (iZone), a program focused on the development of inner-city students. The grant that funded the special curriculum was originally slated for three years, but our department fought for – and received – a one-year extension. I became director in the third year of iZone at a time when the state was threatening to take over the program because students were not performing at an acceptable level. Although the state was evaluating the students' results from years prior to me taking the reins as director, I was told I would be the scapegoat who was left holding the bag for the failing results. Of course, I believed my proven track record of success within the district would afford me every benefit of the doubt, and my seniority would outweigh any attempts to tarnish my reputation. However, I got caught in a tangled web of politics, power struggles, and pride, and when the fourth year of the grant expired, so did my time in the school system.

My superiors reneged on a promise to place me in a lateral position or promote me when the grant expired, even though there were open positions that I was qualified for. Instead, I was repeatedly told in letters from the human resources department that I could apply like everyone else for positions that were essentially demotions. After two decades of consistently moving the district in a positive direction, I was told that there was nothing left for me. I didn't understand it, and immediately after my release, the district went on a hiring spree for all the positions they told me had not received funding yet. The snub made me feel marginalized but there was little I could do about it.

I was a few years shy of hitting my retirement benchmark that would have entitled me to lifetime benefits that employees receive after 25 years of service. I didn't receive the traditional send-off luncheon celebration, a plaque, pen, or even a certificate of appreciation. On my last day, June 30, 2017, my close friends and team members came to my office to say goodbye, but the top school officials were conspicuously absent. I left my keys on the desk, walked out with my possessions in a box and sat in my car in the parking lot and cried. I was hurt, but I knew this was the consequence of not shifting when I was supposed to.

"You stayed there too long," I heard God tell me.

Many of life's seasons have an expiration date. I was trying to outlive my expiration at the school system, and it didn't turn out well. It's like drinking milk past its "Use By" date, and then getting angry when it makes you sick. I had been given warning signs that my time was up when the grant first expired after the third year. But because I believed in the good we were doing in the students' lives, I fought to stay.

Many times, we clutch tightly to people and places, and God tears us away even if we are kicking and screaming as we go. He releases us from a circumstance that is no longer viable and permits us to walk in a new direction. If I had stayed at my job with the school system, I never would have gone on to pursue my doctorate.

I would not have launched my education consulting practice, started my mentoring and life coaching business, or moved on to the next phase of my life.

"Sometimes God has to allow everything to crumble down to ground zero, just so you can start rebuilding," my father once told me.

When I finally had the courage to let everything go, I was convinced that God was shifting my direction, but not changing my ultimate destiny.

When "The End" Happens
Live Anyway
Let Go And Move Forward

- **Embrace Proper Endings.** Letting go can lead to personal growth, achieved goals, and ultimately better lives. Don't stay with what's familiar just because it's comfortable, especially if you're in a bad situation. Walk away from toxic relationships, and run when numb becomes your normal! Merely operating out of routine is not living your life to the fullest. Do not stay in an abusive relationship for anyone's sake; not your children, your church or anyone. If you ever feel like you don't have an alternative, remember that being loyal does not have to come at the price of total self-sacrifice.

- **Salvage The Good.** If you've ever packed up your living quarters and moved to a new residence, then you've experienced the process of sorting your possessions, evaluating them, saving the useful ones and purging what has become obsolete. Likewise, when a season of your life comes to an end, reflect on what was good and worthy of being preserved, and separate the valuables from the rubbish. Cherish the blessings you enjoyed, the knowledge you attained, and the wisdom you gained from every experience, even if it was difficult to endure in the moment. The best part about my marriage is I have two beautiful children to show for it, and I have a host of lessons learned that helped me become a stronger person. Collect all the positive and constructive things from your journey, take them with you, and display them like badges of honor.

- **Find Liberation In Starting Anew.** Starting over is not as scary as it is liberating. If more people knew this fact, then maybe they would be more willing to do it. Sometimes fear is so blinding, we can't see the freedom that awaits us. When I survey my life today and nothing from my old life haunts me, that is amazing. I have peace when I turn the doorknob to enter my home. I remember days when I would sit in my driveway or open the door to my house, but I wouldn't want to go in. I don't walk on eggshells anymore. And if anything in my life today became a violation of my peace, I'd start over again in a heartbeat. If you ever start over one time, then you know you can do it again.

- **Change The Conversation.** Spend more time talking about the liberation than the discomfort. Talk less about the hard part of starting and more about the joy of the process. It's somewhat like going to the gym; yeah, it's hard to get off the couch, but when I get up and exercise, my health is good, I maintain my weight, I meet new people and I start seeing results. Start talking more about what happens on the other side. It's not the process that's hard; but it's the start that is hard. Leaving comfort and stepping into the unknown is the first step, and it's a step worth taking.

SCRIPTURE AND PRAYER

For everything there is a season, and a time for every matter under heaven: ...a time to seek, and a time to lose; a time to keep, and a time to cast away.

Ecclesiastes 3:1,6

Remember not the former things, nor consider the things of old. Behold, I am doing a new thing; now it springs forth, do you not perceive it? I will make a way in the wilderness and rivers in the desert.

Isaiah 43:18-19

Father,

Today I choose to release everything that has held me back from fulfilling my purpose. I release the past, failures and missed opportunities, and I embrace Your grace and power to boldly move toward the blessings You have for me.

Thank You for a changed heart and a renewed spirit that allow me to forget what is behind me and pursue the great things that are ahead. Help me to know that removing people and places from my life does not mean that I hate them; it simply means that I respect myself.

Teach me to reclaim the goodness that occurs in difficult situations, and give me the wisdom to know when a relationship should be salvaged or severed. I know that not all seasons on Earth are meant to last forever, and I will celebrate each day as a gift from You. Amen.

10

When Trials And Tribulations Happen
Find Strength Through Your Faith

Even when God is the One orchestrating the shifts in our lives, each individual person still has to deal with the consequences and conditions of the situation. For me, this truth was evident when I had no money.

After leaving the school system, my income decreased by 75 percent. During that time, I was trying to pay off nearly $100,000 in debt related to my marriage as well as care for my two teenage children. Although I continued to receive a salary from my church, it wasn't long before I found myself in financial trouble.

I didn't know how I was going to cover all of our basic needs. There were days when I watched my children enjoy their dinner; I waited until they were finished and only ate myself if there was enough left over. Other days I searched for restaurants where children ate free or offered "buy two get one free" menu options. Ordering from the dollar menu at fast food drive-thru windows, relying on gas station reward points redemption to get snacks, coffee and gas, and clipping coupons became my norm. We also started utilizing the free and public assistance that was available to us. For instance, I took my son to a public health clinic for a free sports physical that was required for him to play basketball in high school instead of going to our primary care doctor who charges a co-pay for the same service.

There is no shame in any of this. There are millions of people in our country who I consider to be heroes who make ends meet every day under far worse circumstances. The actual shift in circumstance was a huge challenge for me. When major shifts in lifestyle happen, the key is to successfully manage the mental shift and not just the change in financial circumstance. One of the hardest parts for me was adjusting my mindset and letting go of my pride. In my early days in Chattanooga, I had to learn to accept help from the church ladies who took me grocery shopping and bought all my food. After establishing a decade-long reputation of being an affluent professional, I found myself relearning the same lesson. I had to humble myself and reveal to those closest to me that I could no longer do it on my own. In order for me to survive, it was going to require assistance from those who loved me and wanted to be there for me. I had a renewed compassion for those in need; I was accustomed to helping others, and now the tables were turned. Many days I didn't know how I was going to get by, but God provided for me every step of the way through financial support from my family, my church members, and my entire village.

One day I owed a past-due bill to the electric company in the amount of $152. I had already exhausted my seven-day grace period and without the means to pay, I was preparing for the inevitable that my children and I were going to be sitting in the dark. I had never had my electricity turned off and I didn't know what to do. So, I went on a desperate hunt inside my house to find anything of value that could be pawned to cover the bill. I rummaged through drawers and boxes, and I happened upon a little gold chain that was only big enough to fit a toddler's wrist. It belonged to my firstborn. I had kept it since she was a little girl and I was saving it to give to her daughter whenever she had children.

I slid the chain into my purse, grabbed my keys and immediately drove to the pawn shop. When I arrived, I nodded at the security guard as I walked in the door, and the owner of the shop greeted me right away.

"How are you today, Ms. Randolph?" My recent trips to his store were frequent enough that he recognized me on sight. My first visit was shortly after my marriage troubles became public, and I pawned my wedding ring out of anger and spite. My return to the store this day was out of necessity and survival.

"Well, I have something I'd like you to look at for me," I replied. "How much do you think I can get for this?" I placed the chain on the counter and waited for him to assess my item. This was a humbling experience because the possessions that were precious to me were reduced to transactional commodities, and they always appraised below market value. I didn't expect to get much money from such a small chain, because no one could wear it but a child. But I was hopeful that I'd at least get enough to pay a portion of the electric bill.

"Well, you know gold is back in, and it's very valuable these days," he said after verifying that the bracelet was 18K gold. "I'll give you $155."

I was floored. With this cash, I had enough to keep our lights on *and* order a couple of treats for my kids from the dollar menu on my way home. It was hard to let go of the chain because it actually was priceless to me. It was my baby's and I was saving it for my future grandchild. But I was also very happy to drive up to the window at the utility company and say, "I'm here to pay my bill."

That year, I routinely prayed that my son – who was 14 years old and in his peak growing season – wouldn't grow too fast so that he could continue to fit his clothes and shoes. I didn't mind that my children were witnessing our struggle, but I never wanted them to feel desperate. I shielded them from as much as I could for as long as I could. When the time came to bring them totally up to speed, I sat them down for a frank conversation.

"Our lifestyle is about to change," I explained. "We're going to have to make some sacrifices, but I promise we will be okay."

"What kind of sacrifices are you talking about, mom?" my children asked with puzzled eyes and cautious curiosity.

Even though it was very difficult, I leveled with them about our financial status.

"My income is nowhere near what it used to be," I said. "I depleted my savings traveling to Texas when your grandmother was ill, and I no longer have my high-paying job. I promise your basic needs will be covered, but all the extra things like vacations that you're used to won't be happening for a while. I just need y'all to hang in here with me while we make this transition."

My children were awesome during this time. They were very understanding and began voluntarily deciphering between their needs and their wants. They pitched in however they could with small gestures like clipping coupons, and my daughter even offered to get a part-time job. "No, honey," I reassured her. "Your job is to go to school and make good grades." My children knew I always made sure they were taken care of and they trusted that would never change. My daughter was entering college and my son was starting high school the same year. Even with all the financial responsibilities that come along with that, I continued to tell them, "It's going to be alright. We've got this. And God's got us."

I was thrilled the day my daughter found out she'd been accepted to the university of her choice and she'd earned an academic scholarship that paid for 80 percent of her expenses. But my excitement was quickly eclipsed by the look of uncertainty I saw in her face.

"Mom, it's okay. I don't have to go out of town for college. I can go somewhere local and can stay at home."

My daughter understood that I still had to come up with the funds to pay the remaining 20 percent of her expenses. Without that, she'd have no lodging, no school supplies, nor any of the other required essentials she needed to get enrolled. Even on a payment plan, it was going to be difficult to come up with the money every semester. Despite all that, we were not giving up. I refused to let hopelessness dwell in our midst.

"Oh no, ma'am!" I rejected the thought of her not going to the college of her choice and having the traditional experience of living on campus that she had dreamed of. "We are going to do whatever it takes. And you will be a freshman on campus this fall!" I utilized every financial resource to keep my promise. We maxed out the line of credit on student loans, charged my credit cards to their limits and cashed in unused gift cards that my daughter had been saving for years. I was thankful for all of our church members who also graciously offered her gifts as she prepared to leave home for school.

My son and daughter were great kids who deserved the best of everything. During these days of uncertainty, I learned that even though I might not be able to provide them with the most expensive gifts, I could give them love, peace and hope. We weren't eating filet mignon for dinner; we were eating Hamburger Helper. But we were together, we were at peace and we were good.

My village pitched in occasionally, giving and loaning me money when I fell short. But it just wasn't enough, and I never wanted to be a constant financial burden to anyone. Eventually, I made the difficult decision to cash in my retirement. Because I had not reached age 55, I was hit with hefty penalties for the early withdrawal. But I was willing to sacrifice my long-term security for my immediate survival. For so long, I had allowed financial security to override my destiny. I was so dependent on making a six-figure salary, that even though I loved God, I wasn't forced to totally depend on Him for my daily bread until now. It had been 23 years since I had been in a situation where I had no job and I sat alone in my two-bedroom apartment with nothing more than an air mattress and a TV propped up on a storage crate. I didn't think I'd ever be back in a situation where I didn't know if and when I would get my next check.

"I have to put you in a place where you solely trust Me again," I heard God say. "You have to know that I am your only source of strength and security, and no one else can take the credit for where I am about to take you. I just need you to trust Me."

I'm here to say that nothing gets your faith level where it needs to be like a decrease in pay or not having a solid source to rely on for funds. For the entirety of my career, I knew I was getting paid every two weeks. You don't have to have a lot of faith for that!

But I kept trying to give God a different plan – my plans, such as trying to resuscitate a dying church congregation, trying to save a marriage that was beyond repair, and many other instances where I was delaying my destiny.

I admit; sometimes it's hard to reconcile when your desires don't align with God's will. There are times we can't see the direction God is taking us in at all. And honestly, at times it feels like He is taking us in the completely wrong direction. When you're 20 years removed from a situation, it's easy to look back in hindsight to see how your path was divinely ordered. But in the midst of it, when you're walking through a dense fog, it can feel like you've been thrown to the wolves!

Whenever I had these doubts within myself, I reverted back to the principles that sustained me my whole life.

Do I really believe I am in God's hands? If the answer is 'yes,' then I must believe what He promised, that all things are working together for my good.

Sometimes we're tempted to only calculate good things into the "all," and we neglect to include negative things in the equation. I like to think of the example of baking a cake. In order to get to a delicious cake, you add raw runny eggs, baking soda, salt, flour and other ingredients that are not ordinarily appetizing by themselves. But mixed with "all" the ingredients and properly prepared, the end result is a savory dessert that tastes good, smells good, and is incredibly satisfying. Such is life; a delicate mixture of all things in an effort to achieve a pleasant final result.

We can never predict all the trials we will face in our lives. I believe God allows some obstacles to occur in our lives to challenge us and increase our faith. Other trials are rooted in the Enemy's temptations. Regardless of the origin of the hardship, we must look to our Heavenly Father for strength to disarm the weapons – whether physical, spiritual, or emotional – that are formed against us.

At times I feel like I've been on the defense all my life, fighting through attacks on my faith. For example, in my early 20s, my doctors told me I would never be able to bear children due to health issues beyond my control. I rejected that prognosis and pled with God to bless me with the gift of motherhood. My first pregnancy ended in a miscarriage and it crushed me to my core. I could have given up then and accepted the conclusions drawn by the medical professionals. But I believed with all my heart that God would fulfill the desire that was engrained in my spirit. I believed He would give me the strength and capability to carry a child to term.

After years of trying, I finally got pregnant with my first child and ironically jeopardized my own health in the process. I was placed on bed rest twice, my blood pressure was volatile and shot through the roof several times, and my body swelled all over. But with His grace and mercy, I gave birth to a healthy girl. Four years later, a baby boy completed our family.

Sometimes we face challenges that are too immense to wrap our minds around. While writing this book, the entire world was turned upside down. A once-in-a-century viral pandemic, COVID-19, killed hundreds of thousands of people around the world in less than four months and economies tanked in every corner of the globe. In the United States, tens of thousands of people died from the virus and many more were hospitalized. More than 40 million people lost their jobs and the US unemployment rate reached levels not seen since the Great Depression of the 1930s. Families and communities experienced inconceivable loss and, at a time when we needed a unified nation, we were more divided than ever. Prevention and treatment methods for the virus became political fodder, and neighbors developed animosity towards one another for their choices on simple things like whether to wear a mask to help slow the spread of the disease.

At the same time, our country was also walloped with an eruption of age-old racial tensions when police officers killed an unarmed black man named George Floyd. The video of the homicide was broadcasted in its entirety on the internet and sparked world-wild riots and protests against police brutality. Anger, pain and disbelief gushed from society's collective pores as we tried to reckon with feeling helpless in the face of evil.

During these unprecedented days, I tried to practice all the lessons life taught me about dealing with crisis. If you learn how to navigate one crisis – even though they come in different forms, variables, and intensities – then you have gained the ability to navigate through whatever life throws at you. You can give birth in barrenness, you can curtail financial peril, you can survive a global pandemic, and you can find a way to love your neighbor during times of civil unrest. This is the very definition of what it looks like to "live anyway," whatever may betide.

When others look at me, they may see a little bitty woman of small stature. But there is a lot of fight inside of me; a huge heart that is full of resilience. "Where do you get your strength?" I'm often asked. "Where does your resilience come from?"

My answer is simple. My faith.

When I think of all the ways the Enemy has tried to attack me throughout my life, it puts a smile on my face. He actively and persistently tries to assault and destroy our faith every day. One of his greatest weapons is persuasive deceit. He tries to convince us that God is not with us, and that we are not strong enough to endure life's challenging situations or unwelcomed circumstances. He tries to make us forget the fact that the greater One lives inside of us.

But I know the truth. I've fought through too much adversity, I've prayed too many days and nights, and I've overcome too many times even when it made no human or natural sense. God showed up for me and He promises to do it for anyone who will put complete faith and trust in Him. I gather strength from the heroes of faith that appear in the Bible. I am always inspired by the story of the three Hebrew boys who were tossed into the fiery furnace. Even though the fire was turned up seven times hotter in an attempt to punish them, they were not consumed.

Life has a way of turning up the temperature to a level that feels unbearable. But we can go through the fire and not be burned. I appreciate the experiences I've survived because I know I don't have to give up on life because I get fired or I don't have to lose all hope because I receive a scary medical diagnosis. I hate it and it's difficult, but I don't have to die in it. I can live through it. One of the most rewarding feelings of all is knowing that when other people witness you living through trials and watch you standing on your faith, it gives them a beacon of hope to believe that they can do it too.

When Trials And Tribulations Happen
Live Anyway
Find Strength Through Your Faith

- **Don't Expect Instant Deliverance.** There are some storms in life that God is going to let you ride out. He will not deliver you right away from every trial. Don't be angry with God if you do not receive instant relief from whatever troubles you. The knowledge you glean from the experience is valuable. Even though you might hate the pain, you can appreciate the faith and the strength that it births.

- **Leverage Your Power.** You are a fighter. Romans 8:37 tells us, "… in all these things, we are more than conquerors…" These "things" may include sickness, unemployment, relationship struggles, financial difficulties, depression, or any other turmoil. Learn to tap into your power when faced with adversity. Do not back down and accept defeat. Know who you are, stand your ground, and activate your God-given authority. Don't be frightened by the storms of life; instead, be like Jesus and tell them to "be still."

- **Don't Focus On 'Why.'** Many hardships can be heartbreaking and demoralizing. It's natural to sometimes ask the question, *Why is this happening to me?* Sometimes we know our suffering is the consequence of our own bad actions. Sometimes good people go through bad things, even if they've done everything right. Whether you are a person of faith or not, the latter can be an exceptionally difficult idea to reconcile. However, the Bible teaches us that the sun rises on the good and the evil, and rain falls on the just and the unjust. So, it should be expected that **all** people will experience difficulties at some point in life, and we may never know why. I encourage you to reserve your energy for finding solutions to your misfortunes, and focus on winning, not why.

- **Exercise Discipline And Let God Work.** Be still and allow God – Who is all powerful – to show up for you. It requires discipline to wait on the Lord, and submit to a plan that is not your own. I use a multifaceted approach to maintain a sound mind and a clean heart during joyful as well as difficult times. I practice the spiritual discipline of fasting from food once a week to clear my mind of earthly desires, I exercise daily to keep a healthy body, and I read and meditate on God's word every day to feed my soul. It's in these moments that I am best suited to hear the Spirit of God without distraction and receive His unmatched peace.

- **Never Quit.** I've often been told that I'm as stubborn as a bull. But I say, stubbornness has kept me alive. I urge you to be too stubborn to quit. Learn that it's okay to be uncomfortable. If I had never allowed myself to be in uncomfortable situations, then I never would have developed confidence, reached the next level of faith, or arrived at a place where I reject hopelessness. Know that challenging, frustrating, and even upsetting circumstances are not hopeless. Conjure the strength to keep moving in spite of them and never give up.

SCRIPTURE AND PRAYER

No weapon that is fashioned against you shall succeed, and you shall refute every tongue that rises against you in judgment.

Isaiah 54:17

In this you rejoice, though now for a little while, if necessary, you have been grieved by various trials, so that the tested genuineness of your faith—more precious than gold that perishes though it is tested by fire—may be found to result in praise and glory and honor at the revelation of Jesus Christ.

I Peter 1: 6-7

Dear God,

You are a comforter, provider and keeper. I know that all things are working together for my good even when my circumstances don't necessarily feel good. Please show me Your way and reveal the plans You have in store for me. I will trust You and be obedient to Your will.

Thank You for the faith that was instilled in me by my parents when I was a child. It is a privilege to have my faith tested, especially if I can bring glory to You in any way. Thank You for the models You gave me throughout my life to show me that I can overcome any trial that is set before me.

Please continue to guide me each day on the right path. Grant me patience to be still while you do Your work. Remind me continually that Your ways and thoughts are higher than mine, and I may not always understand why things happen the way they do. Even so, I put my hope in You. Amen.

11

When Victory Happens
Praise God And Pour Into Others

When you've walked through the fire and come through whole on the other side, thank God for keeping you. Allow yourself to be used as a vessel to give light and life to others. I think we have an obligation to share with others the strength we have received. I consider it the highest compliment when someone tells me I've helped increase and grow his or her faith. I gain joy from walking in love and encouragement with others who are fulfilling their purpose. In 2019, I started an organization that is a vehicle for me to do that very thing on a regular basis.

SHE® – which stands for successful, healthy, and empowered – is a mentorship and coaching movement that equips girls and women with the tools and building blocks for a fruitful life. Our work includes mentoring and character skills development for girls in K -12 schools, workshops and summits for women in ministry, motivational speaking for large groups, and one-on-one success coaching sessions.

In my first ever SHE session, I returned to a familiar setting – a high school classroom. I carried a box of crafts, props and snacks into the room where 10 teenage girls were waiting for me. We had an hour to share lunch and discuss SHE principles. While standing before this group of young women, I reflected on how much of my adult life had been a battle, a true test of my resilience and fortitude. God provided me with sufficient grace to win the war, and I was anxious to share my treasures and spoils with these girls in the form of knowledge gems and golden nuggets of wisdom.

"I am Dr. Sheryl Randolph, and I would like to introduce you to SHE," I greeted the girls with enthusiastic remarks. "I hope to inject you with confidence and offer practical, everyday tips to enhance your journey in life. My goal is to tap into your gifts and talents, discuss the various issues that trouble you, and offer tools to help you navigate it all. So, let's begin! The first thing I'd like to do is allow each of you to tell me a little bit about yourself."

As we went around the room conducting introductions, I saw young women who displayed an array of characteristics like insecurity, indifference, energy, hope, and even ambition. There was no way for them to predict the challenges they would face in the coming years, but I wanted to connect with them in a way that piqued their interest. I wanted to share my trials and mistakes so hopefully they wouldn't succumb to the same pitfalls. I intended to give them a guidebook and roadmap for the future even if they weren't ready to hear it. And just maybe they would keep it, lock it away in their hearts, and access it when they needed it later.

Because this was a brand-new mentoring program, I wanted to give the girls an overview of what to expect in the coming weeks. "Our curriculum throughout this program will include character-building and life-building topics such as how to communicate effectively, how to select the right people for each season of your life, how to cultivate your self-esteem and how to know your worth," I explained.

"Oh, we're going to like this!" one of the girls said in a very anticipatory tone. "Are you going to tell us about your life, too?"

"Everything we will discuss in these sessions is not just things I've heard about; I will tell you what I know from having gone through it myself," I confirmed.

"You're a mother and you have your doctorate; you look so young! You are living the dream! Are you going to tell us how to make our dreams come true, too?" one girl asked.

"Well, I don't want you to simply follow my path," I responded. "I hope you all can learn from my experiences and then go on to be the best version of yourself." Mentoring these young ladies felt like exactly where I was supposed to be.

I got practice with coaching young people by first guiding my own children. One evening at home, when my son finally accepted the reality that his parents were no longer a couple, he and I had a heart-to-heart conversation. I reminded him that he is not excused from his destiny just because life challenged him in unexpected ways.

"Darwin, the fact is, you are now the product of divorce and you live in a single-parent household," I told him. "Your circumstance may not be what you want, but God will always make sure you have everything you need. What you may be lacking from not having a father in the home, you are gaining from other male role models that God has placed in your life. I am here with you, and we will navigate this together. Even if you have to cry through it, you're not excused or released from all that you are supposed to be. I'm not letting you off the hook!"

He chuckled and said, "Okay, mom, I get it."

"Do you really have it? Say it back to me just to make sure."

"I will be exactly who I am supposed to be; it's up to me," he recited.

"Absolutely, son. So, keep your F.O.C.U.S. Remember that means, Force Out Contrary Unnecessary Stuff."

It was important for me to check in with my children with one-on-one conversations. While boys and girls require different types of nurturing and guidance, their need to feel safe and loved is common. When having similar talks with my daughter, I recalled how we taught her the power of affirmations when she was only a child.

"Do you remember when your father stood you in front of a mirror and prompted you to say, 'I am Sheridan and I am fabulous'?"

"Yes, mom. I remember," Sheridan said.

"It has always been important for us to help build your self-image. Even though our family dynamics are not what they used to be, it doesn't change the truth of the words we spoke over you years ago. Nothing in your life will change your course unless you give it permission. Don't let circumstances or adult issues keep you from being who God has created you to be. Although your father made mistakes, that doesn't negate the good that he contributed to help shape you as a strong young adult. You can grow up to be an independent woman, and still embrace the idea that men are vital in a woman's life. You are and will be an amazing woman."

My children are my greatest accomplishments. I've been proud of them their whole lives but there's something very powerful about receiving an unanticipated call from one of their teachers who says, "You did a wonderful job raising your son, Darwin. He is so thoughtful and kind to his classmates. I just thought you should know he is truly well-mannered and a well-respected young man." Or, "Your daughter is brilliant beyond her years. If I had a classroom full of Sheridans, then I would love coming to work even more every day."

Sometimes after pouring into other people who are not my children, I don't know if my work and expended energy are in vain. But every now and then, I run into a former student, from my days as an educator, who makes it all worth it. For example, when I walked into a car dealership to shop for my daughter's college graduation gift, I was greeted by one of my former students who was the general manager. "Ms. Randolph, you were really hard on me back in the day, but look where I am now," he said with a sense of pride that was contagious. I found myself beaming in delight as I observed the responsible man he had blossomed into. "You probably thought I wasn't listening when you advised me and diligently tried to keep me in line, but I was listening. I paid attention and you made a big difference in my life; it just took a minute for the results to show. Thank you for pushing all of your students to be our best."

I say it all the time: empowered people empower people. Had I not overcome debilitating losses or clawed my way back from depression and public humiliation, I may not have been equipped to help the next person who faced similar devastation. My triumphs have emboldened me to fulfill my purpose. By God's grace, in 2011, I founded Destiny Church of Chattanooga, a non-denominational church that strives to encourage, equip, and empower people to become fully functioning followers of Jesus Christ; I've served as Destiny Church's lead pastor since its inception. In 2018, I founded SKR Consulting, an education consulting practice. I earned a Doctor of Education (EdD) in educational leadership and professional practices in 2019, the same year I founded SHE® organization. Walking in my calling is a gift for which I am eternally grateful.

I don't boast in my own accomplishments, or my own strength, because honestly without God I would have none. He kept me alive and sane enough to reach this point where I can tell my story. I truly believe there were supernatural powers working on my behalf so that I could become an example for others. Many of my life challenges were so painful, I would not wish them on my worst enemy. But I came through them, and I'm not bitter or defeated. My journey is a testament that people can witness and say, "this is how you can overcome the many obstacles life hurls at you. This is how you choose to defy the odds. This is how you march toward your personal victory and become capable of helping others."

I'm aware that some people never recover from their traumatic experiences. Life breaks them beyond repair, and no level of support, counseling or medical attention can bring them back to a healthy mental and physical state. It's a heartbreaking reality that happens every day. But I am here to encourage you to fight for and claim your victory. I declare that you have the ability to choose joy and maintain a happy outlook. Life will continue to happen and new challenges will arise daily, as sure as the sun breaks the horizon every morning. How you respond is your choice. I implore you to practice forgiveness in the face of betrayal, remember you are worthy if you ever feel insecure, and share the path of victory with others once you have found it. *That* is living.

When Victory Happens
Live Anyway
Praise God And Pour Into Others

- **March Toward Victory Every Day.** Psalm 37:23 reminds us that "the steps of a good man are ordered by the Lord: and he delighteth in his way." However, scripture does not teach us that they will be easy steps. You will face uncertainties, doubts and disappointments on your journey, but keep stepping. Each step takes you further and higher. At times you may be tempted to give up, stop or walk away. Don't do it! Victory is in front of you. So instead of throwing in the towel, get up, wipe your eyes and get to stepping!

- **Praise God.** Remember your Father in heaven who is the source of your strength and all good things. Acknowledge Him, obey Him, and trust Him to guide you. A lot of occurrences that people call detours – such as losing a job or a loved one, battling infertility, or going through a divorce – can actually be God's planned pathways that lead you to your destiny. When you arrive at a place of joy and serenity, praise and thank the One who sustained you along your journey.

- **Claim Your Season Of Victory!** Let me tell you, there is nothing like a win. It reminds you that every setback, hustle, and hurt was worth it. Not only is this your time to win, it is your winning season. Claim it. Take your victory lap! When you show up, show up to be triumphant. Show up to make a difference. We are divinely designed to move from one finish line to another in our quest to fulfill our purpose. Celebrate every success, and live in a place of constant victory.

- **Inspire Others.** What value is there in reaching the mountaintop alone? While you are on your journey to victory, bring someone along with you. Reach back, provide a helping hand, share your knowledge and assist your neighbor or the next generation in maximizing their potential.

SCRIPTURE AND PRAYER

And we know that for those who love God all things work together for good, for those who are called according to his purpose.

Romans 8:28

But thanks be to God, who gives us the victory through our Lord Jesus Christ.

I Corinthians 15:57

for the Lord your God is he who goes with you to fight for you against your enemies, to give you the victory.

Deuteronomy 20:4

For everyone who has been born of God overcomes the world. And this is the victory that has overcome the world—our faith.

I John 5:4

Father,

Victory is part of my inheritance and identity in Christ; for that, I offer my sincerest gratitude and praise. Your word teaches that I am more than a conqueror, and I know I have the power to overcome every trial that I encounter.

Thank You for the knowledge that I can do all things through Christ Who strengthens me. Knowing this, I can face unbelievable odds and not give up. As I stand firm, always remind me that You brought me out of darkness before and reassure me that You are faithful to do it again.

My courage to choose to "live anyway" comes from You. Every day, I will refuse to be defeated and I will be a victor, not a victim, of my circumstances. Thank You for bestowing upon me the power and authority to win. In the name of Jesus, I have the victory! Amen.

Acknowledgments

Every book has its own life, and this one is no exception. *Life Happens. Live Anyway.* is the culmination of writing and reflecting on many of my experiences on my life's journey. Fortunately, I have been surrounded by a number of people who have supported and encouraged me throughout this endeavor. Without their significant contributions, this book would certainly not exist. I am so thankful.

First and foremost, I give all praise and glory to God who kept me and blessed me to write my first book. I'm grateful that He trusted me to communicate this message and for the opportunity to inspire individuals to Live, Intentionally, Victoriously Every day.

It is hard to find the words to express my sincere love and appreciation for my family. At some of the most challenging times in my life, your love and support were constant sources of strength. Sharnette, Shanda, and Cersle, thank you for being the most amazing siblings anyone could ever have. Michael, my brother-in-love, and Dameshia, my God-sister, you guys are the best. Although we are all family, thanks for being my friends.

To my amazing parents, W.C. Kenan and the late Bertha Kenan, thank you so much. No matter the season, you have always been there. I love the joy that you get from seeing the dreams of your children become a reality. Thank you for instilling in me the drive to dream bigger, reach higher, and relentlessly pursue all that God has for me. Dad, you are a wonderful example and I hope to make you proud. Mom, there will never be another like you. As you rest with the Lord, know that your presence in my life will never be erased.

Sheridan and Darwin, you are my greatest gifts. I am so glad I get to do life with the both of you. Thank you for teaching me how to love unconditionally, for introducing me to different genres of movies and enhancing my love for basketball. Mom loves you!

Sparka, thank you for always believing "I can do it" and for being there to help me get things done no matter the sacrifice. You are family!

Mother Linda, thank you for loving me and my children unconditionally. We are so blessed to have you in our lives.

Faith Temple Church, thank you for always being there from my childhood to adulthood. You are more than a church; you are family.

My village, thank you for all you do. You all are uniquely amazing. Life is better with you.

I know I can not mention everyone, but to every person who is a part of my life in some form, thank you for journeying with me.

And finally, thank you Destiny Church of Chattanooga. Your love, encouragement, support and prayers have helped me become the pastor I am today. I truly enjoy doing ministry with you and yes, "the best is yet to come for us!"

Made in the USA
Coppell, TX
05 December 2020

43123461R00090